Formula for
in Vietn

Formula for Failure in Vietnam

The Folly of Limited Warfare

WILLIAM HAMILTON

Foreword by
LT. GEN. THOMAS G. MCINERNEY,
USAF (RET.)

McFarland & Company, Inc., Publishers
Jefferson, North Carolina

Library of Congress Cataloguing-in-Publication Data

Names: Hamilton, William (William Alexander), 1935– author. | McInerney, Thomas, writer of foreword.
Title: Formula for Failure in Vietnam : The Folly of Limited Warfare / William Hamilton ; foreword by Lt. Gen. Thomas G. McInerney, USAF (Ret.).
Description: Jefferson, North Carolina : McFarland & Company, Inc., Publishers, 2020 | Includes bibliographical references and index.
Identifiers: LCCN 2019047352 | ISBN 9781476679945 (paperback) ∞
   ISBN 9781476638188 (ebook)
Subjects: LCSH: Vietnam War, 1961–1975—United States. | Limited war.
Classification: LCC DS558 .H355 2020 | DDC 959.704/340973—dc23
LC record available at https://lccn.loc.gov/2019047352

British Library cataloguing data are available

ISBN (print) 978-1-4766-7994-5
ISBN (ebook) 978-1-4766-3818-8

On the cover: Front cover image © 2020 Shutterstock

Printed in the United States of America

McFarland & Company, Inc., Publishers
   Box 611, Jefferson, North Carolina 28640
      www.mcfarlandpub.com

In memory of my father,
William A. Hamilton, Jr.,
the finest man I ever knew

Table of Contents

Acknowledgments

In addition to the senior Vietnam Era officials who consented to do either in-person or telephone interviews and are listed in the bibliography, the author is indebted to Lieutenant General Thomas G. McInerney, U.S. Air Force (Ret.), who served four combat tours in Vietnam; Rear Admiral H. Denny Wisely, U.S. Navy (Ret.), who flew 350 missions over North Vietnam; Colonel Richard Roberts, U.S. Army (Ret.), who served two tours in Vietnam with the famed 101st Airborne Division; Lt. Colonel Robert L. Barker, whose artillery battery was right in the thick of the First Battle of the Ia Drang, and to famed Vietnam War correspondent and author Joseph L. Galloway. All of them applied their considerable Vietnam combat experience to drafts of the manuscript and offered many constructive suggestions.

In the world of academe, an enormous debt is owed to Professor Edward Homze of the University of Nebraska, Professor F. Taylor Peck of George Washington University, Professor Bernard Rubin of Boston University, and to Colonel John B. Keeley, the founder of the Newport Institute. I am also indebted to Admiral Henry E. Eccles for giving me a copy of *Sound Military Decision.* Anything laudable in these pages is the result of their wise and patient counsel. Any mistakes, errors of commission, and errors of omission are mine and mine alone.

In the world of computer knowledge, I am indebted to Patricia Shapiro of Shapiro Book Publishing for her in-depth knowledge of fonts, typefaces, formatting, and for the cover design.

For his wonderful help with pre-marketing, I want to thank Mike Loomis, the author of *My Book Launch Planner.* With regard to McFarland, I want to thank: Dylan Lightfoot, David Alff, Beth Cox, Lori Tedder, Kristal Hamby, Lisa Camp, and Pam Goodman for a great team effort.

Last, but not least by any measure, I am indebted to Penny Rafferty Hamilton, Ph.D., my wife of 48 years who has been my partner through our wonderful marriage and through the many projects in which we have been of help to each other.

Foreword

For Vietnam veterans like myself, longing finally for an accurate history of the Vietnam War as fought in South Vietnam's Central Highlands and in Cambodia, this volume is a refreshing account based on personal combat experience, in-person interviews of many of the war's major figures, and extensive academic research.

William A. "Bill" Hamilton commanded an airmobile infantry company in the Second Battle of the Ia Drang, served twice as the G-3 operations officer for the famed 1st Air Cavalry Division, and was the S-3 operations officer for the 2nd Battalion, 5th Cavalry during the division's incursion into Cambodia.

Very few Army officers have the opportunity to serve with both of their sister services in wartime. Yet, in addition to two tours in Vietnam, Hamilton served two years attached to the U.S. Air Force and one year as a student at the U.S. Naval War College. This book benefits from his multi-service perspective.

For those who have often wondered why the world's finest armed forces were prevented from winning a quick, decisive victory in South Vietnam, or even to reestablish the *status quo ante*, Hamilton's book is a must-read. My four combat tours in Vietnam attest to that!

Thomas G. McInerney
Lieutenant General, U.S. Air Force (Ret.)

General McInerney spent 35 years in the U.S. Air Force (1959–94), including four tours of duty in Vietnam (1963–69), when he flew more than 400 combat missions. He served in top military positions under the secretary of defense and the vice president of the United States. His last active duty assignment was as assistant vice chief of staff, Headquarters U.S. Air Force, Washington, D.C.

Preface

Like so many readers, I used to skip over the forewords, prefaces and whatnot found before the first real page in works of nonfiction. But as I became a writer of books, both nonfiction and fiction, I came to understand the functions of such pages.

So, if the preface is supposed to tell the reader what's inside the book, why not just read the preface and stop? But that would be akin to looking at a skeleton and being left to wonder what the entire body must have looked like.

That said—and before I stop writing in first person and go to the supposedly more scholarly third person in the main body—allow me to say something about the forces that caused this writer to see the world as I do.

I grew up in a very small town in southwestern Oklahoma that produced cotton, peanuts, alfalfa, cattle, and oil. It always seemed a magical and wondrous place. But, prior to December 7, 1941, we did not need to know much about Europe or Asia or even a place called Pearl Harbor, wherever that was.

My growing-up world was akin to what we would come to know as the world of TV's *Leave It to Beaver*, only better. But, as a six-year-old, I shall never forget that Sunday afternoon when my mother drove us to a convenience store called the Blue Goose.

We were just about to drive off with the *Sunday Daily Oklahoman* when a local shoe salesman tapped on my mother's car window, indicating he had something to say.

He said, "Edith, the Japanese just attacked Pearl Harbor!" I didn't know what that meant. But my mother turned pale and had to hold back tears. Small boys who adore their mothers are attuned to their reactions, and I knew immediately that this was not good.

We drove straight home so she could break the news to my father. After that, my parents huddled next to the radio for more news of the Americans killed and wounded, the ships sunk.

Preface

To say the planet tilted on its axis a bit that Sunday would not be off the mark, just as it tilted on September 11, 2001. Somehow, even at age six, I knew the world had changed. For one thing, the anti-interventionist, isolationist movement came to a screeching halt. But I didn't know that at the time. What I did know was that my parents were visibly upset. Somehow, I sensed that my life was going to be changed.

Up to that point, my life had always been "good" in the sense that those around me were loving and kind and good. I really did not know anything about "evil." I could not imagine why those people being called Japanese or Japs would want to hurt anyone. And who were these people called Nazis? I knew about President Roosevelt because my sainted grandmother, Mama Rennie, did not like him. I began to hear other names like Hitler, Mussolini, Tojo, and Churchill.

My parents and Mama Rennie said Christians had an obligation to oppose evil. Mama Rennie gave me a folio-size, illustrated book called *The Book of Battles.* One of the first was the Battle of Hastings in 1066. She suggested, since my first name was William, that I might find William the Conqueror of interest.

She had no way of knowing that she set me on a course that would lead to a career in the Army and a lifetime spent reading and eventually teaching history at the university level.

During World War II, virtually every American got behind the war effort. The evil enemies of World War II were nation-states with names, with infrastructures that could be attacked.

The Roosevelt Administration cleverly got everyone involved in the defeat of an axis of evil that ran from Berlin through Rome and on to Tokyo. I recall scrap drives to collect essential war materials from tinfoil to steel. Virtually everything was rationed. Adults had coupon books needed to qualify for the purchase of even the most mundane items. We children received war stamp books in exchange for the pennies we rounded up to donate to the war effort. We bought war bonds. Hanging from the ceiling of my little bedroom were black-painted balsa wood models of German and Japanese aircraft. Even in centrally located Oklahoma our teachers quizzed us on recognition of enemy aircraft. Gas rationing, tire rationing and the absence of chewing gum, chocolate candy, and nylon stockings made everyone feel they were contributing in some way to the war effort. Later, revisionist historians would write that all that rationing and doing without was a bunch of hooey. But as events in Korea, Vietnam, and the War on Terror would prove, Roosevelt was absolutely correct in finding ways to get almost every American to support our troops in the field, our pilots in the air, and our navy at sea until the forces of evil were smashed completely.

President Roosevelt avoided the paradox of having just part of the nation at war while the rest of the nation was at peace. Yet, despite Vietnam and the horrors of September 11, 2001, America, even in the Age of Trump, never seems fully engaged in its struggles enough to win.

I

Setting the Stage
for Failure

*Man, it seems, is not able to bear the languid rest on
Nature's bosom, and when the trumpet sounds the signal
of danger, he hastens to join his comrades, no matter what
the cause that calls him to arms. He rushes into the thick-
est of the fight and amid the uproar of the battle regains
confidence in himself and in his powers.*
—Alphonse de Lamartine (1790–1869)

"What did you do in the war?" is sometimes asked of parents. In the case of Vietnam, our children and grandchildren also have reason to ask, "If you were in such a mighty force, how come you did not win?"

For those questions there are answers and that is why the research for this book began in 1970. That was shortly after I returned from a second tour with the 1st Air Cavalry Division in Vietnam and Cambodia. For the next nine months, I would be a student at the U.S. Naval War College in Newport, Rhode Island. For those officers who wanted to put in extra time and effort on nights and on the weekends, The George Washington University offered the opportunity, combined with the curriculum of the Naval War College School of Command and Staff, to obtain a M.S. in International Affairs. Back then, many of the key figures in the Vietnam War were still alive and quite willing to be interviewed in person or by telephone by a brash young Army officer seeking answers to his questions.

Selecting a question or questions to be answered for the required master's thesis was easy. Having spent two years of my life being shot at in Vietnam and Cambodia, I wanted to find out how and why the United States was fighting a land war in Asia and why it was lasting so long with the outcome still in doubt.

During those two years that included 57 days in Cambodia, I had the opportunity to command more than one rifle company in actual enemy

7

contact; most notably, Delta Company, 2nd Battalion, 5th Cavalry Regiment. In both Vietnam and Cambodia, I served as the S-3 operation officer for the 2/5th Cavalry. And, up at the division level, I had served as the G-3 operations officer, twice. More importantly, at the rifle-company level, I had taken part in hundreds of combat air assaults—the specialty of the 1st Air Cavalry Division.

While there was little I did not know about the operations of one of the most formidable war machines ever put together by the mind of man, I was relatively clueless as to how and why we found ourselves fighting a land war in Asia.

Along with my brothers-in-arms, I could tell dozens of stories about brave, young Americans carrying incredibly heavy packs day after day while hacking through thick jungles. We could recount numberless acts of courage and kindness on the part of those wonderful young men we had with us in Vietnam.

As a former operations officer of an airmobile infantry battalion, I could tell them about our truly innovative uses of the helicopter to give our side a tactical mobility advantage. As the former G-3 operations officer for the largest and most complex marriage of men and sophisticated air and ground machines (the 1st Air Cavalry Division), I could spend hours discoursing upon the intricacies of maneuvering an airmobile division supported by more than 450 helicopters. In fact, in 1967, I was tasked to author the 1st Air Cavalry Division's Training Manual 350-1, a pocket book on how to conduct combat air assaults.

The American soldiers I walked with, flew with, and fought alongside were wonderful soldiers. The best. Eventually, the equipment our government provided was the finest. We rarely, if ever, wanted for any material thing. The airmobile concept and the tactics evolved by the 11th Air Assault Division at Ft. Benning, Georgia, and proven in Vietnam by the 1st Air Cavalry Division, were brilliant.

"But if all that is so, how did we lose the war?"

How convenient it would be if we had a simple answer to leave our children and grandchildren as to how and why the United States did not prevail in Vietnam. But the pressures that put the United States ground forces ashore in Vietnam are too complex to permit a simple answer. The same holds true in trying to explain the highly unusual way in which the most powerful nation on earth went about using its enormous power in Southeast Asia against vastly weaker opponents.

Perhaps the easiest course is to blame the architects of the United

States intervention in Vietnam as being too idealistic and failing to place the issue of the political orientation of South Vietnam in its proper place among the hierarchy of the interests of the United States. And yet, if one looks at twentieth-century United States diplomatic history, the American intervention in Vietnam can be seen to flow quite naturally from the pattern of United States response to its need to secure itself in an increasingly dangerous world.

Looking at the events of just over half of the twentieth century, one could not help but be aware of two facts: (1) the United States has grown to be the most powerful and richest nation on earth, and (2) the United States has fallen, at the same time, from the most secure large nation on earth to one of the most insecure. Who would have imagined in 1900 that by 1951, George Kennan, one of our leading diplomatists and historians, would be writing, "A country which in 1900 had no thought that its prosperity and way of life could be in any way threatened by the outside world had arrived by 1950 at a point where it seemed to be able to think of little else but this danger." Kennan makes the case that the Allies (except the USSR) really lost World Wars I and II. None of the lofty goals they proclaimed at the outset of each war were realized. While those goals were secondary to the defeat of the aggressors, the costs to some of the Allies were severe.

Great Britain never really recovered from World War I before the ordeal of World War II. France, weakened physically and spiritually, was led by an incompetent general staff to an early defeat. The security goals America sought by defeating Hitler were brought no closer to reality for the United States. In fact, when the USSR gained hegemony over Eastern Europe and became, in time, a nuclear power, those goals seemed even more remote. The dreams described by Woodrow Wilson's World War I rhetoric were crushed by the communist expansion in the wake of World War II.

This realization, once it came, angered Americans. At first, the reaction, rather predictably, was to search for scapegoats rather than to assign error to our own policies or to credit our adversaries with any great foresight. "McCarthyism," as the reaction was called, tried to blame some officials in the State Department or academics in the universities or even the Army for our failures. While the decoded Venona intercepts proved a number of "parlor pinks" and even a few Soviet agents were operating within the U.S. Department of State and some other agencies within the Roosevelt Administration, the macro problem was a shrinking world in which the interests of the United States encountered the results of Lenin's dictum, "We are living not merely in a state, but in a system of states, and the existence of the Soviet Republic side by side with imperialist states for a long time is unthinkable. One or the other must triumph in the end."

Wish as they might, Americans could not push the communist genie back into the bottle. Inexorably, the Soviet Union used the heavy industrial base it squeezed from the labor of its peoples and stole from occupied nations to produce the means to confront the United States with military power around the globe. The growing power and demands of the so-called developing nations only added to the dangers posed by a world already pulled between the interests of the two superpowers. Thus, it is no wonder that Americans were bitter when this second "war to end all wars" began to look like an elaborate prelude to more suffering, and perhaps, to a nuclear holocaust.

Given the less than satisfactory outcomes of World War II and the Korean War, no post–World War II American government felt it could stay in power if it increased the bitterness and disappointment of its people by being the government that allowed another bit of territory or another people to be pulled behind the Iron or Bamboo Curtains.

Given the times in which they were born and the events they experienced, it is little wonder that the men of the Kennedy and Johnson Administrations were drawn toward the contest in Vietnam. As former Secretary of State Dean Rusk remarked,

> My mind goes back to my senior year in college when Japan seized Manchuria. Everybody said to us at that time that it's too far away—it's none of our business and so in a few years I found myself in a uniform in Burma which was even further away. The combination of pacifism and isolationism in the 30s in the West pretty much made World War II inevitable. So, a lot of us in World War II of my age were fed to the teeth with the idea that that war was not prevented.

Other men such as John F. Kennedy, Lyndon B. Johnson, Robert S. McNamara, McGeorge Bundy, Walter Rostow, John McNaughton, and Maxwell D. Taylor were caught in the wake of a hot war that they had not sought and the Cold War that followed it. Like most Americans, they presumed that surely some way could have been found to have averted the holocaust of World War II.

These were strong and able men—sure of themselves and sure of an American special mission in the world. The rhetoric of President Kennedy conjured the vision of a world set straight again by American power both moral and physical. In the early 1960s, everything seemed possible. But, in the real world of geopolitics, Kennedy was beginning to find that great risks accompanied great foreign policy gains. There are signs that he was beginning to realize, as he had in Cuba and Laos, that all policies carry a degree of risk—some worth taking and some not.

So, simply put, this book is about the American military and its major activities and concerns between 1965 and 1968. That period was chosen because in 1965 a major commitment of United States ground forces was made in the hopes of winning or, at least, not losing, a land war in Southeast Asia. And, by the end of 1968, the decisions that might have brought the war to a relatively speedy end or at least to the *status quo ante* had not been taken within a timeframe acceptable to the American public.

Because the author has more evidence about the activities of the United States Army than its sister services, the primary focus is upon the Army.

In fairness to the men and women, both civilian and military, who have been the architects of United States foreign and military policy since World War II and who constructed United States policy toward Southeast Asia, it is necessary to try to show something of the general institutional and bureaucratic dynamics that have been at work during a period in which the United States found itself paradoxically growing stronger economically and militarily and at the same time becoming more and more militarily insecure.

As we shall see, the influence of the military upon the aims of United States foreign and military policy and its execution sank to an all-time low. Indeed, the voice of the military at the national council table became so enfeebled that it could not compete with the self-confident civilian strategists who required the Armed Forces to wage war under unfavorable conditions and without adequate means. Bottom line: The civilian leadership failed to shape a consistent grand strategy that could attain the aims of national policy in Southeast Asia.

The situation in Vietnam was beyond the reach of our political grasp. The United States, although able to topple the regime of President Ngo Dinh Diem, was not able to install a more effective replacement. The effort to save South Vietnam by military means was fatally flawed by a grand strategy that, perforce, had to acknowledge Sino-Soviet military capabilities. Thus, the military strategy of attrition was adopted—a strategy which required more time and patience than Americans were willing to give and was doomed to failure as long as the North Vietnamese forces were allowed the sanctuaries of Cambodia, Laos, and even North Vietnam.

Formula for Failure in Vietnam

When I entered the war zone in 1966, I was a typical hawk but, over the years, the more I observed our Vietnamese allies and the more I reflected upon the impact of the war upon NATO and our other, more vital, military commitments, and the steps that would have to be taken to "win in Vietnam," the more I began to realize that the Army had been given the mission of fighting "the wrong war, at the wrong place and at the wrong time." Nevertheless, I returned to Vietnam again in 1969 because it was my duty as a citizen and as a soldier to do so. The highlight of that second year was the Cambodian operation in 1970. It had little to do with killing and a great deal to do with gathering up the arms and ammunition the North Vietnamese Army was using to wage war in South Vietnam. The Cambodian incursion bought the government of South Vietnam some more time in which to attempt to resume responsibility for the struggle. Those two combat tours also convinced me that the United States, despite the wide use of helicopters, had thrown away most of its technological advantages and had reduced itself to fighting in a most primitive infantry environment against some of the world's finest light infantry. Even so, the United States Army was more than a match for the North Vietnamese Army. Unfortunately, that fact had nothing to do with the real issue which was essentially political. As a soldier, how and why we engaged in protracted ground combat without the advantages we could have enjoyed was a mystery I wished to understand. The answers, however, turn out to be as complex as the fighting was primitive and much different than I had imagined.

Although the United States failed to accomplish its foreign policy objectives in Southeast Asia, the American military, as such, was not defeated. Our soldiers, sailors, marines, and airmen carried out their assigned missions to the furthest possible extent given the restraints placed upon their numbers, methods, and areas of operation. Now, our task should be to learn the lessons of Vietnam.

Defeat has little to recommend it, but since we cannot alter the past, it should be our goal to learn from it and use the Vietnam experience, gained at so dear a cost to maximum advantage.

But there is a hazard from trying to learn from the past. Many of the Vietnam decision-makers were fond of making historical analogies. The most common one was to compare any hesitation to face the communist challenge in Southeast Asia with the appeasement of Hitler in 1938.

It would be another tragedy if the idea of *Dolchstoss* (stab-in-the-back) gained currency as the total reason for the failure of American policy in Vietnam. To conclude that would assign greater weight to the importance of military operations than is warranted by the facts. The errand upon which the American military was sent was unwise and the directions for its accomplishment confused and without military logic. But, in the end, the stab was not in the back—it was right in the front. As some Vietnam veterans are wont to say, "We took every hill but one: Capitol Hill."

The trick is to un-blind ourselves to the mistakes of both civilian and military leadership and make useful their errors. Having done that there is, of course, the danger of trying to find universals in the lessons of Vietnam and misapply them, like the Munich analogy, to unwarranted circumstances. We should be mindful of Mark Twain's advice: "We should be careful to get out of an experience only the wisdom that is in it—and stop there; lest we be like the cat that sits upon a hot stove lid. She will never sit down on a hot stove lid again—and that is well; but also she will never sit down on a cold one anymore."

Events in Iran provide a perfect example of our continuing failure to learn the lessons of the Vietnam experience. President Carter's decision to rescue the hostages by use of military means was just as incorrect as that of President Kennedy who attempted to liberate Cuba and, having made a bad decision, compounded it by denying the military the means necessary for it to have any chance of success. President Carter did not take into account that several hundred Americans were still in Iran at the time of the hostage rescue attempt. Even if the rescue had been successful, the Iranians would have simply rounded up replacement hostages.

Yet, having decided to use military force, President Carter would not allow sufficient force to be employed. Almost every rule in the commando raid rule book was broken. Primarily, the force was too small and without adequate redundancy of transport. Moreover, the classical principle of "unity of command" was violated.

But the military must also share some of the blame. The military allowed its "can do" attitude to overcome sound military judgment. Someone in the military should have insisted on unity of command, on sufficient forces, and on sufficient transport. Had Delta Force commander Colonel Charles Beckwith been given total command and whatever resources called for by sound doctrine, the story of the hostage rescue might well have had a different ending. The operation could well have resulted in a bloodless extraction of the American hostages. It would not have been a humiliating demonstration of military ineptitude. Delta Force, which never got the chance to go into action, was let down by the sister-service aviation elements that were supposed to support it.

Formula for Failure in Vietnam

President Johnson, having made the decision to commit major American forces to a ground war in Southeast Asia, compounded that decision by not giving the military the necessary authority and freedom of action to achieve a military solution. Therefore, the central lesson is clear: our civilian and military leadership must learn to understand the capabilities and limitations of each other. It is especially important that the military offer sound military advice and not permit that advice to be waffled by misplaced loyalty, inter-service rivalry, or promotion-centered dishonesty.

Having been burned in Cuba, Vietnam, Iran and, post 9/11, in Iraq and Afghanistan, there is the danger of overreaction and failing to act when our vital interests are clearly at stake. Just prior to Vietnam, there was concern that the trumpet calling us to battle made an uncertain sound. After Vietnam, there was concern that the trumpet would never sound again.

Perhaps, we have finally ended the 2009–2016 trend toward unilateral disarmament. But no amount of arms will serve us properly unless they are placed in the hands of a civilian and military leadership group which truly understands the nature of their relationship and the proper roles each must play.

In 1965, American ground combat units went ashore in Vietnam. Prior to 1965, the American commitment in South Vietnam, although not inconsiderable, was limited to a military advisory effort plus a large number of non-military projects intended to rally the people of South Vietnam to the support of the government in Saigon. In addition, the United States Air Force, the United States Navy, and the South Vietnamese Air Force were conducting airstrikes in North Vietnam from bases in South Vietnam, from Thailand, and from United States Navy aircraft carriers stationed in the South China Sea. However, as extensive and costly as these activities were in the number of United States personnel and dollars involved, the character of the advisory, pacification, and bombing efforts was on an entirely different order of magnitude than the landing of United States ground combat forces.

World history is recorded by cartographers in terms of shifting boundaries, of territories won and lost. Thus, the putting ashore of certain types of ground forces is an act of national commitment which puts the honor and pride of the committing nation on international display. Once that step is taken, the armies must either "come back with their shields or on them." When a nation is forced to withdraw ground combat forces of a certain nature, either by direct enemy pressure or due to lack of public support at home, the withdrawal can be termed a retreat and the end result can be called a defeat. To understand that, one need only reflect upon the exit of the French from Vietnam in 1954 and from Algeria in 1962.

The beginning date of a war is most often established when the army of one state crosses onto the territory of another state. With the exception of World War II, which began for the United States with the sneak Japanese air attack upon Pearl Harbor, the major wars of the twentieth century began with ground attacks. World War II in Europe began with the German attack upon Poland in 1939. The Korean War began on June 25, 1950, when the North Korean Army invaded South Korea. But the exact starting date for the Vietnam War is difficult to determine.

War was never officially declared and the American involvement was incremental. Indeed, even the landing of United States ground combat forces was done in such a way and by such types of forces that it is difficult to say with precision just which troop commitment crossed the line between war and peace. Perhaps, then, the test should be to establish the point at which the United States so clearly committed its power and majesty to the attainment of certain objectives that failure to attain them would have to be considered a defeat for the United States.

But what is defeat? The United States, in a sense, suffered a defeat at the Bay of Pigs; however, President Kennedy quite correctly interpreted it as a loss of prestige from which he knew a great nation could recover. He also knew the matter was not serious enough to topple his government.

This suggests a test. It might be said, in a democratic society, a defeat is an event or series of events that either topples the existing government or assures its defeat in the next scheduled election. Under that definition, it is necessary then to look backward and fix the point at which the action of that government placed itself at risk. What, in other words, was the "point of no return"?

Adam Ulam, referring to the start of the bombing of North Vietnam, said in his book *The Rivals*: "The Vietnam War, insofar as the bulk of Americans was concerned, began more or less inexplicably in February, 1965." Walter W. Rostow, in his *The Diffusion of Power*, said, "On that day—July 28, 1965—the die was cast." That was the day on which President Johnson announced the dispatch of 50,000 additional combat troops to Vietnam. In this case, it would seem Rostow has the better argument. But what Rostow does not tell us is that on Monday, July 26, 1965, at Camp David, President Johnson went back on his earlier pledge to the Joint Chiefs of Staff that he would mobilize America's reserve forces. While President Johnson's decision of July 28, 1965, committed the U.S. to fighting a ground war in Asia, his decision two days earlier doomed the war effort to failure. Inadvertently, President Johnson sent a signal to Ho Chi Minh that the United States was not committed to a quick win. The president of North Vietnam realized that time (dictators need not worry about public pressure) and demographics were on his side. For Ho Chi Minh, it became simply a matter of inflicting enough casualties on American youth until public pressure would force the Americans to withdraw.

The United States sends huge sums in support of anticommunist governments only to have to write these sums off when the supported governments fail. The United States has sent advisers to both large and small nations and still failed to maintain them against communist pressures. China is an obvious example. We have overflown the denied airspace of a great power such as Russia and when caught at it had to promise to refrain from further overflights. In the less recent past, we sent the Marines ashore to punish smaller powers to recover the property of our citizens. But none of these efforts, whether successful or not, have been viewed as passing the point of no return. Our reins of government have not changed hands as a direct consequence of these adventures or misadventures.

Except in Vietnam. The Johnson Administration involved the United States so heavily in Vietnam that, when his policy failed, President Johnson had to announce his retirement from politics. By so doing, he assured the American body politic and the whole world that the United States would not continue to seek a dictated military solution to the political contest between communists and non-communists in Vietnam. He involved the power and majesty of the United States beyond the point of no return in a situation to which there was no solution short of taking risks which could have set off another world war or of destroying the very society we had undertaken to protect.

The decision President Johnson made after Tet, in March 1968, and the follow-on decisions in the next few months began the winding down of the American effort in Vietnam. It began the leveling off of the American ground force commitment and led to the initiation of a troop withdrawal. It would seem that if the troop strength leveled off and then withdrawal were the solutions to the political crisis in the United States that followed the Communist Tet offensive of 1968, it would then be reasonable to argue that the point of no return was reached back in 1965 with the introduction of our ground forces.

Troop formations have differing characters and they are perceived in different ways. For example, Marines are considered expeditionary forces.

I. Setting the Stage for Failure

An expedition, by definition, is of limited duration to achieve a limited aim. They are part of influence-projection or power-projection forces. Marines are not expected to stay ashore. They are not organized or equipped for staying power. Thus, their introduction carries with it the implication that they will be withdrawn in short order. Airborne formations are somewhat the same. They have many of the same organizational and equipment limitations of Marines. Although they are intended to operate further inland than the Marines, they too have relatively little staying power. Thus, implicit in their introduction is either their timely withdrawal or reinforcement by larger and more self-sustaining follow-on formations.

Therefore, it can be argued that the introduction of a few United States Marine battalions to secure the United States and South Vietnamese aircraft operating out of Da Nang Air Base was not an irrevocable commitment of the power and majesty of the United States past the point of no return. The same can be said, but with only slightly less conviction, of the introduction of the 173rd Airborne Brigade and elements of the 101st Airborne Division into the Central Highlands of South Vietnam in 1965.

It would appear then that the announcement of the plan to deploy the Airmobile Division (1st Air Cavalry Division) in consonance with the decision to introduce a total of 44 battalions into South Vietnam with the possible follow-on of an additional 24 battalions in the next year was the Rubicon of the Vietnam War. Thus, it can be said that U.S. "ownership" of the Vietnam War began, in the classic military sense, in July 1965.

Politicians, bureaucrats, generals, admirals, and private soldiers do not set out to lose wars. Surely none of those involved in the planning and execution of the Vietnam War could have wished for the course it took or the painful results it brought. Nevertheless, it must be admitted that whenever a nation launches a war there will be those who will use the war for advancement and gain. It is a safe assumption that President Johnson did not want to be the first modern U.S. president to lose a war. But, looking back, one wonders how men of intelligence and good intention could have made the series of decisions producing such bad results.

At the bottom line, one must note the loss of more than 58,000 Americans killed in action, 300,000 wounded, and a dollar cost of approximately 150 billion dollars. To that must be added the intangibles of a divided nation weakened in will and military power and caught in the grip of almost runaway inflation.

A great deal has been written about the decision-making process that led to the United States denouement in Vietnam. Thanks to the Department of Defense study of this decision-making process in United States-Vietnamese relations for the years 1954 to 1967 (known as *The Pentagon Papers*) this close-to-the present history has been remarkably illuminated.

However, despite a virtual torrent of writings about how the United States became stuck in the morass of Vietnam, there is surprisingly little in print dealing with these matters in human terms. The men who wrote the intelligence estimates, drafted the position papers, made the key recommendations, and actually made the decisions were, after all, only human. None of them had any special powers of clairvoyance or prescience. Some among them undoubtedly suspected that they might be omnipotent but, if they did, they only reflected the hubris to which some men are prone.

The commitment of United States ground forces to an Asian land war was a momentous decision. What was so compelling about Vietnam that the Johnson Administration would undertake such a seminal step? There seems to be no easy answer except to observe that several personal, institutional, and bureaucratic dynamics came together in 1965 in a convergence of forces to produce a resultant decision that set the stage for failure.

II

An Army in Search
of a Mission

To understand how and why the leadership of the United States Army reacted as it did to the question of Vietnam, it is essential to have an understanding of the traumatic and disturbing events that had troubled the Army as an institution since the advent of the atomic bomb. According to historian Russell Weigley, at the end of World War II, the Army totaled 8,267,958 men and women. By 1947, the Army was reduced to strength of 991,285. In order to accommodate such reductions, a series of reorganizations had to be undertaken:

> As the wartime Army shrank to peace strength in more or less accustomed fashion, its reorganization too proceeded less as an attempt to meet new kinds of international perils than as a conventional postwar effort to assimilate the lessons of the war just ended. Even the unification of the armed forces in 1947 bore this aspect of looking less to the present and future dangers than to the experiences of the last war.
>
> Some aspects of postwar reorganization, in fact, are difficult to interpret even as responses to World War II but appear more simply as preparations for a hoped-for tranquil peacetime.

But the threat to the Army consisted of more than the to-be-expected postwar decline in strength and the resulting reorganization. The greater threat was in becoming irrelevant in the atomic age. After four long years, a war-weary American public yearned for peace. To many Americans, our atomic monopoly appeared to be a military panacea arriving at a time when the collapse of Europe and Asia had placed unprecedented responsibilities upon the United States. Thus, atomic weapons appeared to be a means by which America could supervise a re-building world cheaply and without the need to maintain a large standing Army. Weigley continues:

> Despite the opening of the Cold War, the American Army faded to near impotence after World War II, at least in relation to the country's responsibilities, and scarcely recovered before the invasion of South Korea in June, 1950. A civilian might think

the Army would be happy to have this respite. After all, no one was shooting and the Army was still being paid. However, military professionals do not think or act in ways always fully comprehensible to their civilian fellow citizens.

It would be difficult for those who are not military professionals to understand fully the sense of corporateness felt by those who are. There is, even in an organization as large as the United States Army, a feeling (at least among the professionals or those the Vietnam draftees called "lifers"), a sense of belonging to something larger than one's self. That something cannot be seen or touched, but it is there. Although many organizations and groups within our society have certain bureaucratic drives, not the least of which is self-perpetuation and enlargement, there is something special about the way a military force feels about itself and *needs to feel about itself*. This is especially true of the United States Army.

Being a soldier involves many hardships. Most people do not enjoy the exposure to cold, heat, disease, family separations, low pay, and the physical hazards that go with peacetime simulated combat. Even among professional soldiers, the psychic satisfaction of being one of the *real* warriors or having a macho self-image wears thin overtime.

But for all the hazards and discomforts of military life to be borne over a full career, there must be the satisfaction of doing something important for the nation. Active combat is not necessary to achieve this satisfaction. Indeed, preserving a peace favorable to the United States is a much more commonly held good among the professional military. To soldiers it is important to belong to an organization playing an important role in the life of the nation. Without that self-concept, soldiering is a difficult, often stultifying and occasionally dangerous career. Thus, in the late 1940s, the Army yearned for a *raison d'être* that would not be just a quick fix for the current crisis but would endure regardless of whatever weaponry was currently in vogue.

So deep was this urge to find a permanent and important role in the defense structure that not even the Korean War (which was primarily an Army operation supported by air and sea forces) provided sufficient reassurance to the Army to still the unease it felt since Hiroshima and Nagasaki.

But there was much in the Korean experience that should have given the Army heart. The failure of the Air Force to interdict the flow of communist supplies to the front argued that airpower alone could not be decisive. While the Navy was largely effective in sea control operations around the Korean Peninsula, it and the Marine Corps could not have mounted the massive ground operations necessary to stop the communist ground drive against South Korea. As historian Russell Weigley points out, "the Korean War gave a new sense of purpose to the Army, and made possible a sort of Army renaissance." The Korean War made it possible, but the renaissance did not take place.

Unfortunately for the Army, while Korea proved the absolute need for a viable Army, in a political sense the war was a setback for the soldiers. The unpopularity of the war caused a reaction in government that flew in the face of the Korean War experience and increased the fears of the Army to near paranoia. The echo of the last rifle shot had hardly faded when Secretary John Foster Dulles announced a "new look" in American policy, replacing limited war with massive retaliation. Now the Army was back to square one. What followed in the middle and late 1950s was another series of strength and money cutbacks.

Massive retaliation was an instant hit with the public. The Air Force ostensibly became the leading edge of the defense establishment, with the Navy to have a strategic role someday with its nascent Polaris submarine fleet. The Army, once again a Cinderella, went back to counting each piece of coal in its bins, while it hoped for better days. By 1958, money was so scarce for the Army that some officers and NCOs had to chip in to buy toilet paper, or soap for the mess hall and wax for the barracks floors. Maneuver funds were almost nil. Resentment for President Eisenhower grew because he seemed, even to the trooper in the barracks, to have turned his back upon the old drab Army from which he had come, to embrace the boys in blue and their shiny strategic bombers.

There was resentment at the top as well. The Army leadership in the 1950s, while it had to live with its reduced role and budget, put up a strong fight to press for a relevant role. General Matthew B. Ridgway, who became Army chief of staff on August 16, 1953, soon found himself in conflict with the "bigger bang for a buck" philosophy of Secretary of Defense Charles E. Wilson. Wilson felt that the United States Air Force offered the bigger bang. Ridgway, always the model soldier, did his best to alert his civilian masters to the dangers of having insufficient ground forces to meet challenges short of nuclear war. He never went around his bosses to the press or to the president. Only under direct questioning by congressional committees would Ridgway permit himself to detail his differences with the party line of the Defense Department. He had little success in his efforts and elected to retire after two years as Army chief of staff. In 1956, he published a memoir titled *Soldier*, which revealed his fears for a United

States trying to contain the communist challenge with what he felt were inadequate ground forces.

Soon to follow Ridgway into retirement was Lieutenant General James Gavin, the Army's brilliant chief of research and development. Gavin felt the Army had a valid role in long-range missile weaponry that was being denied by the Air Force and by the Department of Defense. Outlining the Army's case in his *War and Peace in the Space Age,* Gavin pressed his attack upon the Eisenhower, Dulles, and Wilson reliance upon massive retaliation while excluding the Army from playing its logical role with surface-to-surface missiles.

General Ridgway's successor was General Maxwell D. Taylor, a gifted soldier-scholar who shared General Ridgway's apprehensions. Taylor served two, two-year terms as army chief of staff but made no more headway than did his predecessor in carving out a more relevant role for the Army. In 1959, one year after his retirement, General Taylor published *The Uncertain Trumpet,* which caught the fancy of the junior senator from Massachusetts, John F. Kennedy. Kennedy read history avidly and took more than a passing interest in military affairs. The unhappiness of such redoubtable soldiers as Ridgway, Gavin, and Taylor made an impression upon Kennedy who, as a presidential hopeful, was no doubt looking for alternative strategies to those espoused by the party occupying the White House.

Ridgway, Gavin, and Taylor were very much in accord in their desire to stake out a relevant role for their service. Taylor, however, turned out to be the most effective spokesman with what he called "flexible response." Later, Taylor proved to be too flexible for Ridgway and Gavin who felt United States military power was not unlimited and that certain areas such as Asia were inappropriate for the deployment of United States ground forces. As we shall see, Taylor would split over this issue with Ridgway and Gavin who fanned the heart of the so-called "Never Again Club" which was opposed to the use of United States ground forces in Asia unless, of course, it was absolutely vital to United States security to do so.

Undoubtedly, the three generals had their problems with the civilian leadership in Washington; however, their problems rested chiefly upon obtaining money to support the Army's participation in the task of defense. The generals who would follow them would find money easier for the Army to get, but they would have far less to say about how it would be spent.

III

Beware of the
Pale Civilian

By law, "the Joint Chiefs of Staff (JCS) are the principal military advisers to the President, the National Security Council, and the Secretary of Defense." In 1965, however, as President Johnson approached his decision to commit United States ground forces to fight in Vietnam, he did not make full use of the professional military counsel available to him. But Johnson's reluctance to seek military advice from uniformed professionals was in accordance with a trend begun with the National Security Act of 1947, which at once finalized and circumscribed the powers of the JCS and the individual service secretaries.

To some degree, the Joint Chiefs of Staff brought this reduction upon themselves due to a natural tendency on the part of each service chief to serve the interests of his own service, sometimes to the detriment of the overall defense establishment. The central concern of the Joint Chiefs of Staff was the growing military power of the Soviet Union. Quite naturally, each chief felt his own service should play a leading role in meeting the communist challenge. Inevitably, disputes arose from time-to-time. As a result, it was said around Washington, "the Congress debates, the Supreme Court deliberates, but the Joint Chiefs bicker."

In time, the Congress and the president agreed to strengthen the power of the secretary of defense in an attempt to smooth out inter-service rivalries. In 1953, that was done by taking the JCS out of the chain of command so that it ran from the president to the secretary of defense through the civilian service secretaries to the commanders in the field. In 1958, the service secretaries were removed from the chain of command. The JCS were given operational responsibility for the unified and specified commands. But actual orders descended from the president to the secretary of defense to the unified and specified commands deployed around the globe.

It should be noted that the orders of the commander-in-chief and/ or the secretary of defense go *through* the Joint Staff, which the secretary of defense uses as his military staff. Although the chairman of the Joint Chiefs of Staff outranks all other officers of the Armed Forces, he may not exercise military command over the Joint Chiefs of Staff or over any of the Armed Forces. The Defense Reorganization Act of 1958 reduced the role of the service chiefs and the military departments to suppliers of soldiers, sailors, airmen, and marines to the unified and specified commands for use as directed by: (1) the commander-in-chief and (2) the secretary of defense—both civilians.

The 1958 Act increased the scope of the chairman's duties making him the spokesman for the other chiefs to the secretary of defense and the commander-in-chief. Presumably, the chairman would present the joint view of the chiefs and, when there were unresolvable differences, he would try to be the honest broker of the divergent view or views to the secretary and president (General Earle G. Wheeler, who died in 1975 at age 67, carried the burden of honest broker for six difficult years.) In addition, the new law put a formal restraint upon free and easy communication between the service chiefs and the Congress. In effect, the chiefs had to defend official positions of the Department of Defense and could state their views only under direct questioning while testifying before congressional committees. Any of the Joint Chiefs of Staff could go around the chairman and the secretary directly to the president if they wished; however, courtesy and military custom would require them to inform the chairman and the secretary of defense prior to taking such action. Therefore, free communication with the president was inhibited by this chain of command.

By 1960, the stage was set for Robert McNamara. Seizing the initiative and armed with the requisite legal authority and the unqualified backing of President Kennedy, Secretary McNamara began to bring all activities in the Defense Department under his own control. Central to the effort was Mr. McNamara's conviction that "the direction of the Department of Defense demands not only a strong, responsible civilian control, but a Secretary's role that consists of active, imaginative and decisive leadership in the establishment at large, and not the passive practice of simply refereeing the disputes of traditional and partisan factions."

McNamara's first steps changed the rules by which decisions about military strategy and procurement were made. To do this, McNamara brought into his office a staff of systems analysts. McNamara and his staff felt that the generals and admirals relied too much on their judgment and experience as a basis for decisions. The generals and admirals felt that some things just could not be quantified and had to be decided on the basis of judgment and experience. Over the McNamara years, the battle centered on just where this fine line lay.

Technology favored Mr. McNamara. The computer and communications revolutions allowed the secretary of defense to gather information about almost every aspect of the Armed Services. Commenting on the conflict between the military and management, John B. Keeley at the University of Virginia said,

> The management procedures imposed on the military by civilians are less the result of a conscious attempt to undermine military expertise than they are the almost inevitable consequence of improved means for information gathering which permits higher authorities in every kind of organization to pervade nearly every activity at almost every level. The information dredge which scours the organization at all levels for more and more information also erodes the basis of authority for subordinate leaders.

Nor was the burgeoning technology of the new information industry all that influenced Mr. McNamara. His own background, his rise to power in the Ford Motor Company conditioned him to think in management versus labor terms. As secretary of defense, he and his civilian staff were the "managers" of the armed forces, while the people in uniform were the "labor" element, the senior officers being analogous to foremen. (This failure to understand and respect the real nature of military people was later to make for confrontation where before there had been mutual trust, confidence, and loyalty. The McNamara perception, plus the tendency to downgrade military service from a profession to an occupation, led some to talk of unionizing the military.)

Authority shifted in the McNamara Pentagon from the generals and admirals, who had spent their lives as practitioners of military and naval science, to a group of young civilians armed with only unending questions and the business machines to process rapidly the answers to those questions. The struggle over who should make decisions and how they should be made was difficult enough, but to that was added a degree of personal animus. The generals and admirals could scarcely conceal their contempt for McNamara's "whiz kids" and McNamara and his civilian colleagues had little respect for the military. As Robert W. Berry, who served in the office of McNamara's general counsel and later served as general counsel for the Department of Army put it:

Formula for Failure in Vietnam

Not only did the Secretary substitute his judgment for the military advice given him, but also his subordinates did. We saw the growth, of course, of systems analysis, first under the Assistant Secretary of Defense Comptroller and, subsequently as a separate Assistant Secretaryship. But this was not the only place within OSD that the staff started to operate almost independently of the military. The International Security Affairs area is another place in which there was a strengthening of that shop, and it was relied on probably more than the Joint Staff during the early days. Thus, the Secretary involved himself in weapons acquisition, strategy, and perhaps even tactics. This, of course, was a whole new ballgame for the military. It was the first time that a Secretary of Defense had asserted that he had authority in every aspect of the Department of Defense. The obvious effect of this was to, in the opinion of many, downgrade the military. My analogy is simply that for the first time the military forces were commanded by a civilian Secretary.

General Theodore R. Milton, who worked closely with McNamara as the Air Force adviser to Commander-in-Chief Pacific (CINCPAC), said

McNamara has an almost blind faith in facts and figures. He had a notebook just full of facts. He knew everything. You could, scarcely tell him anything. And he would argue with you. He would challenge you and say "my figures don't back that up" and then you would have to explain to him why his figures weren't exactly the right answer. He didn't have much use for us. I don't think he thought we were nearly as bright and able as he and his gang were.

Despite the clash of viewpoints and the personal leadership styles, the military eventually had to try to make peace with the solidly entrenched McNamara. As John B. Keeley pointed out:

For a short while in the mid–1960s, the Services and the Office of the Secretary of Defense attempted to define a comprehensive set of rules, to determine who made what decisions. Some progress was made, and financial limits to obligational authority were established at various levels. But in the broadest sense the pulling of decision authority to higher and higher levels (within the Services as well) was one of the most profound consequences of the McNamara management system. The resistance of the Services to this pull created the tension, very powerful in those days, which exists even to the present.

The outcome of this struggle was vital to the future roles the generals and admirals were to play. For the systems analysts the contest was not as crucial. Systems analysis had proven itself to be a useful management tool, and its future was assured. The future was not so certain for senior military officers because if almost everything could be quantified and rationalized mathematically, then generals and admirals were simply anachronisms in every regard except for holding command in the field. If intuitive judgment and professional experience were to be relegated to a minor role in the decision-making process, then generals and admirals are not needed anymore at the highest levels of the defense establishment because it is primarily for their judgment and experience that they hold positions in the defense staff.

But, to the Army, the appearance of McNamara paradoxically brought new money and new hope. President Kennedy ordered Secretary Mc-Namara to survey the strengths and weaknesses of the defense establishment. After a rapid study, McNamara reported the United States had a significant edge over the Soviets in strategic weapons but had little capability to respond to communist threats in situations short of total war. To Kennedy, this was unacceptable. He could not accept a situation in which his choices were "holocaust or humiliation." Impressed with the writings of Chairman Mao, Che Guevara, and other revolutionaries who used guerrilla warfare successfully, Kennedy determined the United States must develop the capability to deal with what the communists were calling, "wars of national liberation."

Obviously, the Army would have to play the lead role in this new policy. This turn of events was pleasing to the leadership of the Army and especially so to retired General Maxwell D. Taylor, who had just been appointed to serve in the White House as Kennedy's personal military advisor. Armed with an expanded mission, new money, equipment and friends in the White House, the Army leadership had one more hurdle to clear—how to get along with Robert McNamara.

Service chiefs who crossed McNamara did not last long. Admiral George W. Anderson Jr., the chief of naval operations, was sent to Portugal as United States ambassador after he challenged McNamara on his ill-fated TFX or F-111 all-service fighter plane. The fact that Anderson was correct made no difference. By the time the TFX flopped, Anderson was long gone.

General George H. Decker, the Army chief of staff, welcomed President Kennedy's interest in the Army and the infusion of funds it would bring. Unfortunately for Decker, he did not share with the president and Secretary McNamara the same ideas as to how the new money should be spent.

General Decker's responsibilities made him mindful that the Army had to be prepared to conduct more than just counterinsurgency operations. The Army had a commitment to defend the rolling plains and wooded forests of Western Europe, it had to be ready in Korea in case of another conventional invasion, and it had to maintain a strategic reserve against overt aggression by the Sino-Soviet Bloc. Kennedy, on the other hand, was keen on counterinsurgency and the expansion of the Army's Special Forces or Green Berets. General Decker did not share the President's enthusiasm for the Green Berets, and Kennedy sensed it. Also, Decker did not project the snake-eating image Kennedy admired so much. Decker, an excellent golfer, had more the demeanor of a corporate executive or financier. In fact, General Decker was a fiscal expert who was not awed especially by Secretary McNamara's dexterity with numbers. On top of that, Decker was one of the service chiefs who had been on board at the time of the Bay of Pigs fiasco. Even though the Joint Chiefs were only marginally at fault on the Cuban misadventure, all these factors combined to make Kennedy wish he had someone more to his liking as Army chief of staff.

To open the post of Army chief of staff for a new appointment, President Kennedy dispatched his military aide-de-camp, Major General C. V. Clifton to call upon General Decker. General Clifton began the conversation by asking General Decker if he would like to be reappointed Army chief of staff or become an ambassador. Since the customary procedure when the president wanted to reappoint a service chief to a second two-year term was for the president himself to ask the incumbent if he desired a second appointment, the signal from the commander-in-chief through Clifton was subtle, but clear. General Decker, however, did not want to be reappointed. He was 60 years old and his wife was not well. He had decided on his own to retire. Thus, in a sense, he was not fired by President Kennedy; however, it is equally clear that had he wanted to stay on that he could not have.

Although President Kennedy displayed some degree of sensitivity in his approach to removing General Decker for a general more to his liking, the actual mechanics of General Decker's retirement revealed McNamara's lack of understanding of traditional military values or perhaps just a callous indifference to the sensitivities of those under him. General Decker, although he had conveyed his desire to retire to President Kennedy through Major General Clifton, did not know when he was to retire. A number of general officer shifts were to be made and the matter of timing was, of course, the prerogative of the president. The plan was for General Lyman L. Lemnitzer, the Joint Chiefs of Staff chairman, to replace the retiring General Lauris Norstad as the Supreme Allied Commander Europe (SACEUR). General Maxwell D. Taylor was to be recalled from retirement to become chairman of the Joint Chiefs of Staff. General Earle W. Wheeler was slated to replace General Decker. Suddenly, McNamara feared the press was about to break the story of these general officer changes before they could be announced by the government. Calling Cyrus Vance (who was then Secretary of the Army) to his office, McNamara directed Vance to make a press release announcing these personnel changes by 5:00 p.m. EST that day. Vance inquired if the principals involved knew about these changes and learned that General Decker had not been told when he was being retired. Vance protested to McNamara that the chief of a military service should not learn of his retirement from a press release. McNamara then directed Vance to go tell General Decker that he was retiring immediately, only to learn that General Decker was on an inspection trip in Panama. Next, McNamara told Vance to telephone Decker and give him the news. Again, Vance protested that a telephone call was not the way to tell a service chief that he was being retired momentarily. Exasperated, McNamara ordered Vance to fly to Panama and tell General Decker in person. Within an hour, Vance was aboard a special jet for Panama.

Succeeding General Decker was General Earle G. Wheeler, a big, strapping man whom Kennedy had liked when Wheeler had been detailed to brief the then presidential candidate on military matters. Wheeler was a former mathematics instructor at West Point. Conceivably, he would not get confused when McNamara and his whiz kids began to move numbers around on the budget sheets.

When Air Force Chief of Staff General Curtis E. LeMay scarcely concealed his contempt for the whiz kids and McNamara's gradual approach to the bombing of North Vietnam, he was extended for only a one-year second term, rather than the normal two-year term.

In fairness, it should be noted that removing service chiefs was not an original invention of Kennedy, Johnson, and McNamara. President Truman offered his Chief of Naval Operations, Admiral Louis Denfeld, the choice of a less prestigious post in the Atlantic or dismissal when Denfeld told the House Armed Services Committee "that Administration policies were severely weakening the Navy in favor of the Air Force and the Army." Another Truman appointee as CNO, Admiral William Fechteler, got his job, in part, because he was the only four star admiral not involved in the 1945 "revolt of the admirals," when the Navy brass fought to keep the aircraft carrier fleet from being replaced by the B-36 bomber.

The Eisenhower chiefs had their share of troubles. In order to rid himself of the Truman-appointed Admiral Fechteler, Eisenhower dispatched him to be Commander-in-Chief Allied Forces, Southern Europe. Ridgway and Taylor left their service as Army Chief of Staff unhappy and frustrated because of the backseat mission and low funding given to the Army. General Lemnitzer was pushed aside for his role in the Bay of Pigs and for complaining that McNamara was not giving the joint staff enough time to study problems posed by the secretary of defense. Also, he was moved to make room for President Kennedy's favorite—General Maxwell D. Taylor.

It is interesting to note that General LeMay was the last of the members of the Joint Chiefs of Staff during the Kennedy and Johnson Administrations to depart under a cloud. Thus, from January 1965 through the Nixon Administration, no service chief failed to be reappointed for a second two-year term unless he was appointed to be the chairman of the Joint Chiefs of Staff or died in office.

To officers aspiring to be a service chief or chairman of the Joint Chiefs of Staff, the lesson was obvious. There was a need at the top for flag officers who could get along. Those who were argumentative or too closely bound to a particular service viewpoint went out.

Secretary McNamara, in support of the strategy of flexible response, rearranged the priorities in the defense establishment.

The strength of the Army rose from 858,622 in 1961 to 1,066,404 by 1962. In addition, the Air Force produced more airlift capability to carry the Army to the next war and began to show a grudging interest in providing close air support to the ground forces. The Navy was given new sailing instructions that stressed the capability of moving the Army and resupplying it by sea.

For the Army, the Kennedy era was the best of all possible worlds. Down at the troop level, the salutes had a new snap, a sense of pride and a feeling of being once again in the front rank of the Cold War team reawakened. The United States Army in Europe, with new money for equipment, gasoline, and maneuvers, increased its combat readiness. Under the command of General Bruce C. Clarke, practice alerts were frequent and realistic. All officers and men had to be off the street by midnight or they answered to General Clarke. Clarke was a bear of a man who could freeze an errant subordinate with a stare. He was also compassionate in his way, feeling that the way to take care of a soldier was to make him tough and ready. Thus, Clarke allowed little time to enjoy the delights of Bavaria. Clarke's hard-nosed approach was to pay off as the Cold War grew more heated. (Moreover, indiscipline, drug abuse and racial tension were virtually unheard of in the hard-training army of General Bruce C. Clarke.)

When Soviet Premier Nikita Khrushchev tried to force the Allies out of Berlin in 1961, Kennedy's stand was backed by an alert and ready United States Army in Europe. In 1962, during the Cuban Missile Crisis, Kennedy not only had a strong force deployed forward in Western Europe, but also had a formidable strategic reserve in the United States called Strike Command, which was under the direction of another fire-eating Army General, Paul D. Adams.

How long the United States Army, Europe, and Strike Command could have maintained their keen edge cannot be judged. After the Cold War tensions lessened in 1963, and after the departure of General Bruce Clarke, began to relax. The midnight curfew was lifted, more time was allowed for enjoyment of family and club activities. Slot machines appeared in the NCO and officers' clubs, but despite the lessening of tensions, the Army in Europe remained ready. But the real problems that were to come to the Army in Europe had little to do with creature comforts and curfews. The decline of the Army in Europe would be ordained by events far away—in Hanoi, Saigon, and Washington.

By the time Lyndon B. Johnson became president, Robert Strange McNamara had done what official Washington had long thought impossible—he was managing the defense establishment. He stood atop the most powerful war machine in history. With the strongest backing from both Presidents Kennedy and Johnson, he dominated the Pentagon as no civilian secretary had ever done. Defense funds flowed from the Congress through his hands to the military services. From the commander-in-chief came his authority over the military. He controlled what they bought and what they could do with it, and if not what they thought, he at least controlled the channels they would have to use to oppose him.

In the ordeal that Lyndon Johnson would face, he would need the wisest of counsel but he, as President Kennedy, would not see the need to receive advice on military matters directly from military men. His civilian secretary had been able to produce a great and flexible force and he would look to his civilian secretary for advice on how to employ it.

"Up or Out"

If the senior officers were having their problems, the junior officers trying to become senior officers also had to face some internal adjustments within the Army. The Army installed a new promotion policy called "up or out." It meant that just being a career officer was not sufficient to permit one to serve 20 years to qualify for a half, base-pay retirement. In essence, the new regulations said that if an officer failed twice to be selected for promotion to the next higher grade he would be put out of the service. For those with less than 18 years of service, this meant no retirement pay at all.

Thus, for some officers, the greatest good became making the next promotion. Because the number of positions to be filled at each higher grade became increasingly fewer, the new policy meant that many fine, efficient officers would be pushed out of their careers by those whose Officer Evaluation Reports (OERs) reflected that they could "walk on water."

The Army's OER system was based upon a two-part subjective rating by one's immediate superior and the rater's superior. A third officer reviewed the report, but only to check that it is administratively correct. Thus, an officer had only to impress two supervisors at any given time with his ability to get his job done without getting the tops of his shoes wet.

Obviously the up or out system tends to generate officers who will concentrate, to the exclusion of other matters, on impressing the two superior officers who matter most to their promotions. Unfortunately, when there are a limited number of promotion vacancies, this system can and does eliminate many officers of high character.

Officers who do not show any sign of fear in combat have been reduced to jelly at the thought of being forced out of the Army short of retirement. Many Army skills have no civilian counterpart. A former soldier without civilian skills or additional education could have a hard time feeding or educating his children.

Despite a lot of breast-beating about "Duty, Honor, Country" and integrity, the fear of being passed over for promotion led to lying, cover-ups, false reporting, and obedience to the desires of the rater and endorser even though what they may direct might be illegal, immoral, or even criminal. (The deeper ramifications of this problem will be discussed in Chapter VII, but in examining the actions of the Army from 1965 to 1968, the external and internal pressures which had been at work on and within the Army from the advent of the atomic age through the period of Vietnam should be kept in mind.)

A less obvious, but tremendously important, evil caused by the up or out system was the perversion of the traditional "can do" attitude of the Army. Giving each task the old college try is commendable. But if the leadership becomes so corrupted by fear of being passed over for promotion that it says "can do" to an impossible task and then covers up failure to accomplish the task, with false reporting, a serious breakdown in the fiber of the leadership or organization involved takes place. In the environment of up or out it became increasingly difficult to find staff officers or commanders who could say "can't do." Thus, the Army as the reflection of its collective parts, found itself willing to say "can do" to an inappropriate mission in Vietnam.

The Defense Intellectuals

Clemenceau's famous aphorism raised the question about the importance of war and to whom its conduct should be entrusted. Even in Clemenceau's time, politicians and generals contested over this function. A rather grim prospect in the minds of many. However, had Clemenceau lived to see the post–World War II period, he would have had to make a judgment about a new group of contestants—the defense intellectuals.

With the advent of the atomic bomb, the continued existence of the world became so problematical that some of the brighter minds of academe began to devote a great deal of attention to strategic thought. Some offered their advice and prescriptions from within the halls of ivy, while others went to work for the nascent think tank industry. Basically, the latter became hired minds whose chief employers were the military departments. Thus employed, they debated and wrote about the merits and demerits of massive retaliation. They developed specialized vocabularies to describe the events they envisioned in almost unending scenarios depicting the moves and countermoves of the superpowers and their attendant and smaller non-nuclear nations.

When Soviet atomic strength grew sufficiently strong to raise grave doubts about the practicality of massive retaliation, the emphasis shifted to exploring alternative strategies such as limited war and flexible response.

Although most of the defense intellectuals were in the universities and the think tanks, the Army had its own rather respectable strategic thinkers. Generals Ridgway, Taylor, and Gavin, as mentioned earlier, were quite adept at articulating their support of alternatives to "massive retaliation."

Not all defense intellectuals remained outside the government. Indeed, it was not uncommon for them to flow rather freely between academe and actual government service and back. Another order of this priesthood could be found in business and in defense-related industries. Many of these industries, in fact, developed think tanks and war gaming facilities of their own. Those who came into the government from whatever source tended to be men who liked to solve problems rather than just theorize about them.

President Kennedy was extremely successful in attracting into his government some exceptionally bright problem solvers. Although they might differ in social origin, academic credentials, and political orientation, they shared one common trait: they believed almost any problem, if properly analyzed, was capable of an American solution. These were men of the New Frontier. There was no Augustinian fatalism for them. To them, the United States had a mission in the world. President Kennedy's exposition of this theme in his inaugural address struck a chord with such men when he stated, "Let every nation know, whether it wishes us well or ill, that we shall pay any price, bear any burden, meet any hardship, support any friend, oppose any foe to assure the survival and success of liberty."

Thus to address the question of the survival and success of liberty in Vietnam, the United States had in its service many bright and able men eager to execute the mandate of their President. In the White House were McGeorge Bundy, Walter W. Rostow, and Michael Forrestal. A few blocks away in "Foggy Bottom," the State Department had Dean Rusk, William Bundy, and Roger Hilsman. Across the Potomac in the Pentagon were Robert S. McNamara, John McNaughton, and General Maxwell Taylor.

Unfortunately, among this array of talent were men who, given the power and position in government to do so, could not resist the temptation to try out some of their pet theories. Walter Rostow and General Maxwell Taylor are good examples. They, along with Dean Rusk, had the idea that they could modify the behavior of the men in the Hanoi Politburo by the gradual application of military and other pressures. The goal they sought was to make the leadership of North Vietnam desist in its efforts to reunite Vietnam under its communist government. (But why did these men feel their goal possible of attainment when the United States was having so little success making a Jeffersonian democrat out of President Diem and his successors?)

Of the three, Rostow was the most disposed to urge a wide variety of courses of action which leapt to his agile mind through the process of his extremely wide reading of history. At one time Rostow decided it was important to bomb the Petroleum Oil and Lubricant (POL) storage sites in North Vietnam. He got this idea from reading how badly such action had hurt the German war machine in World War II. Despite intelligence analysis pointing out that North Vietnam's POL needs were so minuscule that bombing would not have any significant impact upon their military operations, Rostow persisted until the missions were flown.

Walter W. Rostow and John McNaughton are excellent examples of defense intellectuals who seemed to believe that bright people could solve any problem and that lack of previous experience was no obstacle to their making the effort. Air Force General Theodore R. Milton, who accompanied Rostow and General Taylor on their mission to assess the Vietnam situation for President Kennedy, said about Rostow:

> Rostow was an idea man. [Although] he had never been in the Pacific at all ... he said: "I have an idea. The first thing we've got to do in Vietnam is seal off the border between Vietnam and its neighbors." I said, "That's absurd we can't do that. You'd just have to see it [the jungle] to believe me." He said. "Why you can do anything if you want to do it. You know this is what we've got to do." I said, "Well, in the first place the only people in the world who know where the border is between Laos and Vietnam, for example, are people like you and me. They don't know it, those people out there. It is a jungle."
>
> Of course, he got out there and changed his mind a little bit, but this idea persisted and in the end turned into this "McNamara Line"—the electronic fence and all the rest of it. They were idea men. There is nothing wrong with having ideas, but what were they trying to do? This was dilettantism.

Commenting on John McNaughton from McNamara's office, General Milton said,

> McNaughton was terribly arrogant and contemptuous of the military. I have never seen anybody show his contempt so thoroughly as he did. He used to come to these meetings at CINCPAC every few weeks. Very bright, very prolific, he could sit down and do the minutes of the meeting in nothing flat and make them read very nicely and see that the right ideas were in there, but it was really a dilettante approach.

Evidently, the multilingual soldier-scholar General Maxwell D. Taylor was not intimidated by the defense intellectuals. One evening, General Taylor, General Milton, and Professor Rostow had dinner together while Taylor pondered what recommendations to make about Vietnam. As General Milton recalled,

> It was that evening, sitting there at dinner, that I think he [Taylor] decided that he was going to recommend that we have a "command" in Vietnam, "MACV." Rostow was there, Rostow kept horning in with names, "so and so would be perfect for it," he said. And finally, Taylor said, "Look, you don't know anything about this. You can't understand what we are talking about. Please be quiet. We are talking about organization, not personalities."

Formula for Failure in Vietnam

The struggling governments in Saigon were deluged with the bright ideas of the well-meaning doers in Washington. When Maxwell Taylor was United States ambassador in Saigon, he sometimes felt the Government of Vietnam (GVN) would sink under the weight of good ideas from the Potomac. Perhaps no one in Washington understood how thin the veneer of leadership in the GVN was. In fact, just meeting visiting American senior officials at Tan Son Nhat Airport with officials of appropriate rank practically stripped the GVN autocracy of talent.

During the brief Kennedy Administration, the defense intellectuals in government found willing allies among the Army planners who delighted in President Kennedy's emphasis upon counterinsurgency and nation-building to counter Sino-Soviet troublemaking in the developing countries. Just how far President Kennedy would have pursued the effort to shore up the GVN will never be known, but the new doctrines seemed to take on a life of their own. As Michigan University history professor John Shy noted, "They have not only underpinned foreign policy; at times they have themselves created foreign policy, as in 1964–65, when the existence of military force and a doctrine for its employment seemed to move into a vacuum of informed and constructive political thinking."

Undoubtedly President Johnson wanted to demonstrate to the New Frontiersmen that he too could move in the area of foreign affairs. For that reason alone, it is doubtful that Johnson could have assigned to the problem of Vietnam less interest than that given by Kennedy. Some say President Kennedy would never have gotten the United States into an Asian land war. Others, who lay equal claim to knowing the fallen leader's mind, say otherwise. This is one of history's imponderables, but clearly President Kennedy's death provided another element in the dynamic process of going beyond the point of no return.

Many of the defense intellectuals Kennedy brought into the government remained after his death. Some of them would stay for the course of the war. Others, after pushing for increased involvement in Southeast Asia, returned to academic pursuits and then, as time went on, became bitterly opposed to the war. This prompted Robert D. Heinl, the military analyst of *The Detroit News*, to complain that "it is in Vietnam that the rearguard of a 500,000 man Army is numbly extracting itself from a nightmare war the Armed Forces had foisted on them by bright civilians who are back on campus writing books about the folly of it all." Were he around today, Georges Clemenceau might want to add to his list of those to whom war should not be entrusted.

Zion of the Nuclear Wilderness

In 1963, Vietnam was not the biggest problem confronting President Johnson, so it moved along in the care of those who were most interested—the defense intellectuals and the military. Slowly, the American investment in money, advisers, and material reached considerable proportions. Increasingly, American blood was spilled as the Viet Cong grew increasingly determined to oppose the work of the American advisers.

It was not only American blood, however, that deepened the American commitment. The United States could not avoid a certain moral responsibility for the death of President Diem and his brother. The United States had seriously interfered in the internal affairs of another state and thus it could be argued had some responsibility to see that the affairs of the South Vietnamese were somehow made better than before the American intervention.

By 1964, Hanoi was concerned that the increasing United States effort in South Vietnam would make the almost moribund Saigon government more difficult to bring down. Thus, in 1964, the NVA/VC launched a series of raids against GVN and United States installations. These raids provoked the United States to retaliate by bombing targets in North Vietnam. This active combat role caused the arrival of more Americans and more combat aircraft to be based in South Vietnam. As the numbers of aircraft grew, concern for their security began to build pressures to bring in American ground troops to secure them. Thus, the North Vietnamese and the United States began to step up the symbiotic moves and countermoves that raised the level of violence in South Vietnam. This eventually led to General William Westmoreland's call for American ground combat troops to come ashore in Vietnam.

At the start of 1965, the curtain was about to go up on the acts that would irrevocably entwine the United States with the fate of South Vietnam. Consciously and unconsciously, internal and external pressures were mounting upon and within key officials and their organizations to put United States ground troops ashore in Vietnam.

The Army was moving inexorably toward a demonstration of its *raison d'être*. The McNamara realignment of the defense effort was producing the means to support an aggressive foreign policy. The Joint Chiefs of Staff were adjusting to the rules of the McNamara Pentagon. The Army, with the best of intentions, had adopted personnel policies that began to exert enormous pressures upon its members to produce optimistic estimates and reports about whatever their superiors wished to hear. The defense intellectuals produced attractive limited war and flexible response strategies that promised release from the straitjacket of massive retaliation. The defense intellectuals inside the Kennedy and Johnson Administrations pushed their own pet theories about the gradual application of military power to make lesser states compliant. Both Kennedy and Johnson, following in the tradition of the Truman Doctrine, wanted no more dominoes to fall into communist hands. The guilt over the death of Diem and the paralysis after the death of the American president served to move the Johnson Administration along the path of more, not less, effort in Vietnam. Finally, the U.S. investment grew so great that it either had to be withdrawn or protected.

For the Army, the temptation was irresistible. Before it lay a mission short of atomic war and the chance to prove that ground armies were not obsolete. It was the Zion for which the Army had been searching ever since it began to wander through the nuclear wilderness in 1945. The U.S. Army was ripe to bite the forbidden fruit of an Asian ground war.

IV

A War in Search
of Strategy

*A number of ill-conceived and risky ventures undertaken
by Athens give further pause. There is not enough evidence
to charge the demos with the responsibility for the inaus-
picious expeditions against Cyprus and Egypt. But when
we turn to the conception and execution of military plans
during the war, the role played by the masses stands out
more clearly. The Sicilian expedition furnished a particularly good example. The plan itself, as has been argued
earlier was rational enough. But it probably was not discussed with the open-mindedness and self-criticism which
was demanded by the immense scope of so grandiose an
enterprise. In fact, Thucydides reports that the debate was
so dominated by emotions that it was not safe for those
opposing it to express their views lest they be suspected of
a lack of patriotism.*
            —From *Thucydides and Politics of Bipolarity*
                                    by Peter J. Fliess

It is easy to look back upon United States policy toward South Vietnam and say they backed the wrong government in a land far away and
in which the vital interests of the United States were not at stake. But,
the apparent challenge to the United States posed by the efforts of North
Vietnam to reunite Vietnam under a communist government could not be
seen so clearly by the Kennedy and Johnson Administrations. Indeed, it
was terribly difficult for the Nixon Administration to extricate the United
States from Vietnam even after the enormity of the error of our involvement had become obvious to most informed observers. Nevertheless, just
because a task is difficult or because an issue is complex, does not excuse
poor performance by those who lead a great power. Indeed, the errors of
the past should have excited interest in their examination with a view toward improved stewardship of American power in the future.

Formula for Failure in Vietnam

In reviewing the United States policy toward Vietnam in the 1960s, it is useful to examine it in the light of some sort of normative model. The model chosen for use here was first published by the United States Naval War College in 1936 in a book called *Sound Military Decision*. Under a heading called, "The Advisory Function," this book, which was the "bible" for students at the Naval War College prior to Pearl Harbor and throughout World War II, attempts to set out a model relationship between civil and military authorities in the coordination of national policy with the power to enforce it.

> Understanding between the civil representatives of the State and the leaders of the Armed Forces is manifestly essential to the coordination of national policy with the power to enforce it. Therefore, if serious omissions and the adoption of ill-advised measures are to be avoided it is necessary that wise professional counsel be available to the State. While military strategy may determine whether the aims of policy are possible of attainment, policy may, beforehand, determine largely the success or failure of military strategy. It behooves policy to ensure not only that military strategy pursue appropriate *aims*, but that the work of strategy be allotted adequate *means* and be undertaken under the most *favorable conditions*. [Italics mine.]

Using the above, for the sake of examination, as an ideal civil-military relationship, one can look at United States policy toward Vietnam in the light of several questions which can be extrapolated from this model. They are:

1. What measure of understanding existed between the civil representatives of the State and the leaders of the Armed Forces?
2. Was professional counsel available to the State?
3. Were the policy aims of the United States such as to enhance the effectiveness of military strategy?
4. Conversely, was the military strategy the correct one to accomplish the aims of policy?
5. Were adequate means allotted to support the strategy?
6. Was the strategy undertaken under favorable conditions?

An attempt to answer these particular questions was the focus of a research paper prepared by the author for the Naval War College in 1971. Briefly, that study concluded: "the Kennedy and Johnson Administrations saw neither the need for, nor the virtue of, independent, *professional*, military advice on policy matters which were fundamentally military in nature." Former Army Chief of Staff General Harold K. Johnson felt the charter issued to the Joint Chiefs of Staff by President Kennedy and reissued by President Johnson to include social, political, economic and other considerations was in error. Although General Johnson had no objection to the consideration of those elements, provided that the military advice was not compromised by the consideration, he was concerned that further erosions of the military considerations would take place during the decision process to the detriment of the final military solution. Ultimately, the chief executive, with the assistance of the National Security Council, must sort it out.

The availability of wise professional counsel has already been addressed in the preceding chapters to the effect that such counsel was available, but could not be delivered effectively and undiluted by civilian interpretation to the commander-in-chief because of the increased powers of the Office of the Secretary of Defense, the powerful personality of Robert S. McNamara, and the probably unrealistic honest broker role assigned by law to the chairman of the Joint Chiefs of Staff. But it should be kept in mind that there is no acid test (other than the outcome of a war) to determine just how professional was the military advice available to any administration.

The secretary of defense and the commander-in-chief are entitled to their own opinions as to the worth of advice they receive from any quarter. Rightly or wrongly, President Kennedy felt he had been let down by his military advisers on the Bay of Pigs and that they were too eager to attack Cuba during the Cuban Missile Crisis.

President Johnson, according to Hugh Sidey, who covered the White House for *Time*, reported in his book, *A Very Personal Presidency*, that President Johnson was deeply suspicious of military men.

> He found them contemptuous of new ideas, mean and thoughtless in dealing with those below them. He detected an alarming amount of sheer stupidity which was self perpetuating because of the academy caste system.... In fact, the general level of competence which Johnson found among the admirals who came before the Naval Affairs Committee convinced him that the nation could not put its complete trust in the military in such hazardous times. This lack of confidence in the officer corps never really left Johnson.

McNamara's condescending attitude toward the military was not improved when he asked the Joint Chiefs of Staff to tell him how much the 1966 Joint Strategic Operations Plan (JSOP) would cost if he supported all their requests. They had no answer.

Four questions are yet to be addressed and that will be the purpose of this chapter and those that follow.

To Win—An Idea with Many Meanings

First: What were the aims of United States policy in Vietnam?

Only four days after the assassination of President Kennedy, his foreign policy advisers pressed the new president to address formally the question of Vietnam. Thus, President Johnson's first important decision was to approve National Security Action Memorandum 273 (NSAM) which began,

> It remains the central objective of the United States in South Vietnam to assist the people and Government of that country to win their contest against the externally directed and supported communist conspiracy. The test of all U.S. decisions and actions in this area should be the effectiveness of their contribution to this purpose.

However, what did it mean "to win the contest" in the context of a struggle which was so uncertain in its nature and about which the United States government, in 1963, knew so little? It should be noted that NSAM 273 does not speak of an invasion of South Vietnam. Indeed, the exact form the threat to South Vietnam was taking remained unclear for quite some time and then one's understanding of it would depend upon one's point of view. For example, if one were a member of the anti–French Vietminh and also a communist, one might not perceive of Vietnam as being divided into a North and South. In all probability, such a person would see only one Vietnam in the throes of a revolution designed to deliver Vietnam from foreign domination and to allow it to be unified as an independent communist state. Thus, there could be no South Vietnam to invade and the Saigon government, which was non-communist, would have to be considered illegitimate.

On the other hand, if one were a Vietminh, but not a communist, one would see the problem in essentially the same way except the desired result of the revolution would be an independent, non-communist Vietnam. Again, Vietnam would be seen as one country; however, it would have to be conceded that the direction (and as time went on, much of the manpower) stemmed from Hanoi and that third countries were being used as supply routes and *sanctuaries.*

If one were a communist Vietminh, but willing to admit to the de facto division of Vietnam into two portions as agreed upon by the Geneva Accords of 1954, one would not speak in terms of an invasion but the use of force to reunite the country in lieu of the never-held elections which were to accomplish reunification.

Finally, if one were a non- or anti-communist Vietminh and visualized Vietnam in terms of the Geneva Accords, then one would see a North and a South Vietnam divided until such time as elections could be agreed upon between Hanoi and Saigon to determine how and upon what basis the two Vietnams would be reunited. Under this circumstance, one would have to interpret the insurgent actions of the Viet Cong as an illegal interference in the processes of the South Vietnamese government and people. Later, when North Vietnamese Army (NVA) units began to operate in South Vietnam, that would have to be considered as an invasion. This last view was the one with which the United States allied itself.

Two other Vietnamese perceptions are worth noting. Among the more sophisticated South Vietnamese, there were a considerable number who wanted freedom from France in an evolutionary fashion. They did not want a revolution because they did not think Vietnam capable of operating as a modern country without some relationship with France. In fact, about 250,000 Vietnamese were members of the French Army that fought the Vietminh. This group, because of their love for France and its democratic institutions, had little choice but to ally itself with the aims of the Government of Vietnam (GVN) and the United States.

Secondly, there were the provincial Vietnamese who were non-ideological and concerned only with life in their villages. Tragically, they were the majority of the people—caught between competing forces they could not easily comprehend.

Given the complexities of how even those living in Vietnam might perceive what was happening, it is little wonder that the United States found it extremely difficult to have an informed opinion and to formulate a coherent foreign policy toward that divided land. The imprecision of United States objectives in Vietnam plagued the Johnson Administration from its very outset. There is evidence that President Kennedy, who was more at ease with foreign policy matters than President Johnson, was not certain just how far he would go in shoring up the South Vietnamese government. He had given up on one South Vietnamese government (Diem) and, from that, one would have to recognize the implication that he might someday give up on the entire venture.

Winning Hearts and Minds vs. "Find the Bastards and Pile On!"

At the time of President Kennedy's death, the United States involvement was limited to an advisory effort, and that effort was torn between those who wanted to develop counterinsurgency forces to meet the threat and those who wanted to mold the Army of Vietnam (ARVN) to fit a more conventional and more familiar mold.

Lieutenant General William P. Yarborough, one of President Kennedy's favorite generals and the officer who presided over the expansion of the United States Special Forces, argued that the United States Army had an institutional bias against unconventional warfare because it was more familiar and thus more at ease with the large, road-bound, conventional formations designed to defend against Soviet expansion on the plains of Western Europe. Ambassador Robert Komer, who headed the pacification programs for Generals Westmoreland and Abrams, argued that it was not that we were unaware of the unconventional steps necessary to win the hearts and minds of the South Vietnamese to the GVN, but that those who wanted to do those things could not overcome the institutional drives of the military, the State Department, and other bureaucracies that had long traditions of doing things in conventional ways.

> Molding the Vietnamese forces in the mirror image of the U.S. forces, which were supplying and training them, was another natural institutional reaction. We organized, we equipped, we trained the ARVN to fight American style, with American weapons and American tables of organization and equipment, using American ammunition, because this was the only way we knew how. Those who pointed out that this was not quite the answer were up against the ineradicable institutional dynamic which made their advice, however sensible, utterly unacceptable to an organization which was unable to accept that advice operationally, even if it comprehended it intellectually.

General Yarborough points out that embracing the unconventional approach could have adverse career consequences: "a lot of people are afraid to put themselves out on a limb. If it's too far away from the norm, then they're afraid somebody on that—that general's promotion [board] is going to say this guy's a crackpot. For God's sake don't—don't put him on the list."

Major General Charles. J. Timmes, who served in 1961 for eight months as deputy to the Chief of the United States Military Assistance Advisory Group (MAAG) in Vietnam and thereafter, until 1964, as Chief of the Vietnam MAAG, recalled:

> General Taylor's recommendations were almost totally couched in conventional warfare terms. During [his] initial visit [October 1961] the main emphasis was to provide the ARVN forces with additional Table of Organization and Equipment Units (TO&E) and to equip them pursuant to a modified (US) TO&E Table. He recommended (as I recall) initially organizing and equipping three additional

IV. A War in Search of Strategy

Infantry regiments: 46th, 47th, 48th and after that to organize two additional Infantry divisions 9th and 25th. In addition, the existing ARVN units were to be brought up to full TO&E standards. Emphasis ... was in building up conventional formations and their equipment. The conventional units were to be trained in counter-guerrilla (CG) warfare but actually little thought and much less under-standing was given to guerilla warfare. As to why—we just simply did not under-stand CG warfare and we expected to deal with it by conventional means.

Even though JFK, as the commander-in-chief, was so keenly inter-ested in counter-guerrilla warfare, very little was done to prepare the ARVN to deal with this rather old, but to the modern American military new, form of combat. General Timmes recalled,

In simplest terms, from 1961 to 1964, we did not understand guerilla warfare or how to counter it other than by conventional means. The training did include such gimmicks as defense of an attack on fortified villages—how to setup an ambush and how to avoid or counter an ambush—defense of strategic hamlets and seeking out VC infrastructure in the hamlets. We never (at least in those early years) had a counterinsurgency doctrine.

The example of the French defeat in Vietnam should have stimu-lated interest in not repeating the mistakes of the French. One look at the burned-out hulks of the armored vehicles of Groupment Mobile 100 that decorate Mang Yang pass on Route 19 between An Khe and Pleiku should have been lesson enough.

On the other side, there are convincing arguments that the ARVN needed to be organized, equipped and trained to meet the conventional threat posed by the NVA. General Westmoreland said:

I elected to fight a so-called big-unit war not because of any Napoleonic impulse to maneuver units and hark to the sound of cannon but because of the basic fact that the enemy had committed big units and I ignored them at my peril. The big unit war was in any case only a first step. As a former member of my staff in the Penta-gon, Lieutenant General Richard G. Stilwell, wrote later, in likening insurgency to a boulder, a sledge first has to break the boulder into large fragments; groups of work-ers then attack the fragments with spalling tools; then individuals pound the chips with tap hammers until they are reduced to powder and the boulder ceases to exist.

Walter Rostow opined, "It was an exceedingly complex, multilayered war and became progressively a conventional war without a fixed front—almost completely so after Tet 1968 when the VC were permanently damaged." In the conclusion to *The Lessons of Vietnam,* authors W. Scott Thompson and Donaldson D. Frizzell observed:

there is great irony in the fact that the North Vietnamese finally won by purely conventional means, using precisely the kind of warfare at which the American

Army was best equipped to fight.... In 1975, when the North Vietnamese Army planted the flag of victory atop the presidential palace in Saigon, its spokesman made clear that it was they who had won the war. In their lengthy battle accounts that followed Hanoi's great military victory, Generals Giap and Dung barely mentioned the contribution of local forces.

The outcome of the war might have been the same no matter what type of forces were used or how they were used because of basic flaws in our grand strategy. However, there is the possibility that the counter-guerrilla approach envisioned by President Kennedy might have reduced the cost of the war to the United States and thus permitted greater latitude in the dimension of time—a dimension that would, in the end, prove critical.

"Assurance of Winning"

It is interesting to note that NSAM 273 [National Security Action Memorandum] spoke of assisting the South Vietnamese "to win their contest." War is essentially a contest. There is some question to be decided by force. If the successful resolution of the question is absolutely vital to one of the contestants, that contestant has no choice but to employ any and all means available to attain the objective. If the question is not absolutely vital to the viability of one contestant, that contestant may elect to expend less than maximum effort. How much less can be expended and still win depends upon an accurate assessment of the enemy's capabilities and an understanding of just how vital the outcome of the contest is to the other contestant. The United States chose to limit the amount and kinds of power it would expend in the contest and it should be kept in mind that the United States had woefully inadequate demographic information about the Vietnamese coupled with an inadequate understanding of the drives impelling the North Vietnamese leadership. We failed to appreciate the historic enmity between the Vietnamese and the Chinese. Since the outcome of the contest is already known, one would have to conclude that the United States either involved itself in a contest which was not vital or it underestimated the amount of effort required to win, or both, or that it could not win except at the risk of greater interests.

On the morning of July 2, 1965, Secretary McNamara asked General Wheeler to assess "the assurance the U.S. can have of winning if we do everything we can." That afternoon, the late John McNaughton, Chief of International Security Affairs for Secretary McNamara, sent a memorandum to General Wheeler's assistant, General Andrew J. Goodpaster, in which McNaughton attempted to define winning in Vietnam:

> One key question, of course, is what we mean by the words "assurance" and "win." My view is that the degree of "assurance" should be fairly high—better than 75% (whatever that means). With respect to the word "win," this I think means that we succeed in demonstrating to the VC that they cannot win this, of course, is victory for us only if it is, with a high degree of probability, a way station toward a favorable settlement in South Vietnam. I see such a favorable settlement as one in which the VC terrorism is substantially eliminated and, obviously, there are no longer large-scale VC attacks; the central South Vietnamese government (without having taken in the Communists) should be exercising fairly complete sovereignty over most of South Vietnam. I presume that we would rule out ceding to the VC (either tacitly or explicitly) of large areas of the country. More specifically, the Brigadier Thompson suggestion that we withdraw to enclaves and sit it out for a couple of years is not what we have in mind for purposes of this study.
>
> At the moment, I do not see how the study can avoid addressing the question as to how long our forces will have to remain in order to achieve a "win" and the extent to which the presence of those forces over a long period of time might, by itself, nullify the "win." If it turns out that the study cannot go into this matter without first getting heavily into the political side of the question, I think the study at least should note the problem in some meaningful way.

The authors of the *Pentagon Papers* commented upon the contents of this memorandum:

> The McNaughton memorandum is of interest because it demonstrated several important items. First, the fact that the question about assurance of winning was asked indicates that at the Secretary of Defense level there was real awareness that the decisions to be made in the next few weeks could commit the U.S. to the possibility of an expanded conflict. The key question then was whether or not we would become involved more deeply in a war which could not be brought to a satisfactory conclusion.
>
> Secondly, the definition of "win," i.e., "succeed in demonstrating to the VC that they cannot win," indicates the assumption upon which the conduct of the war was to rest—that the VC could be convinced in some meaningful sense that they were not going to win and that they would then rationally choose less violent methods of seeking their goals. But the extent to which this definition would set limits of involvement or affect strategy was not clear.

By the time of McNaughton's memorandum of July 2, 1965, the United States already had 15 combat battalions either in Vietnam or en route, and a total force level of 75,000.

It was rather late to be talking about "assurance of winning"; however, the ground combat forces committed to that point (with the exception of one battalion of the 1st Infantry Division) were all either airborne or marine battalions. Presumably, one could claim that due to the expeditionary nature of marine and airborne forces that an irrevocable commitment of the power and majesty of the United States had not already been made, but such a case would be quite thin. If the United States had not crossed the Rubicon of either victory or defeat by the time the secretary of defense was wondering what assurance the United States had of winning, it was certainly crossed when President Johnson opened a press conference on July 28, 1965, by saying, "I have asked the commanding general, General Westmoreland, what more he needs to meet this mounting aggression.... I have today ordered to Vietnam the Air Mobile Division and certain other forces, which will raise our fighting strength from 75,000 to 125,000 men almost immediately. Additional forces will be needed later, and they will be sent as requested."

Another interesting portion of the McNaughton memorandum indicates that the secretary of defense had fallen way behind the situation on the ground in Vietnam. Since March 1965, General Westmoreland had an ever-increasing number of United States combat battalions in Vietnam. Initially, the first arriving battalions were limited to close-in security of airbases in South Vietnam, but by June 1965, General Westmoreland had requested and received permission to use the forces he had to seek out and engage the enemy if it was "necessary to strengthen the relative position of the GVN forces." Obviously, General Westmoreland could not maneuver his forces without giving them some sort of mission. It was equally obvious that their missions would have to devolve from some sort of overall strategy for their employment. General Westmoreland envisioned the use of the forces he had and those to follow in three phases:

The first phase involved arresting the losing trend, stifling the enemy initiative, protecting the deployment of our forces, and providing security to populated areas to the extent possible. I estimated that this phase would carry through to the end of 1965. In the second phase, U.S. and allied forces would mount major offensive actions to seize the initiative in order to destroy both the guerilla and organized enemy forces, thus improving the security of the population. This phase would be concluded when the enemy had been worn down, thrown on the defensive, and driven well back from the major populated areas. The third phase would involve the final destruction of the enemy's guerrilla structure and main force units remaining in remote base areas.

A basic objective in each of the three phases was to cut off the enemy from his sources of supply—food, manpower, and munitions. Simultaneously, pressure would have to be maintained against all echelons of the enemy's organization—main forces, local forces, guerrillas, terrorist organizations, and political infrastructure.

IV. A War in Search of Strategy

If one compares McNaughton's conception of winning, i.e., to convince the enemy that he is not going to be able to win and thus induce him to choose less violent methods of seeking his goals with General Westmoreland's three-phased concept of operation, it is clear that the framers of grand strategy in Washington were talking about causing the enemy to *desist* while Westmoreland, the framer of military strategy in the field, was talking about *defeating* his opponents.

Commenting upon this apparent contradiction, Dr. Amos A. Jordan, who served in the ISA (International Security Affairs) under John McNaughton, said:

> It may be asking the military to do something it is incapable of doing—to have two different war objectives—at the senior (macro) level and at the junior (micro) level.... It makes the senior military have to face, Janus-like in two directions. It puts a tremendous burden upon the JCS to have to try to make military sense out of the Grand Strategy of making the North Vietnamese desist. To do that the military would have to be allowed to deploy their forces and operate them in such a way that would make total defeat of the enemy possible without violating the constraints placed upon military action by the Grand Strategists.

By allowing the VC and the NVA forces to retreat, without pursuit, into the sanctuaries of Cambodia and Laos, where they could rest, refit, and be resupplied, neither the *desist* nor the *defeat* objectives had any chance of success.

General Maxwell D. Taylor, in a series of lectures delivered at Lehigh University in 1966, stated that President Johnson's speech in Baltimore in April 1965 was a succinct statement of United States policy. According to Taylor, "Our objective is the independence of South Vietnam and its freedom from attack. We want nothing for ourselves, only that the people of South Vietnam be allowed to guide their country in their own way." He went on to cite a second United States objective, "to prove that this new technique [wars of national liberation] can be stopped and can be defeated; and having defeated it, we can participate in transforming Southeast Asia into a peaceful, prosperous area free from external threat. In such a transformation, a North Vietnam which adjures aggression will find an honorable peace."

It should be noted that President Johnson said nothing about defeating the North Vietnamese. The thrust of the president's statement was that the United States aim was to secure the independence and freedom of the people of South Vietnam, but the implication is clear that the United States would have to cause the North Vietnamese to desist from those activities which prevented the attainment of the United States aim. General Taylor used the word *defeat* to describe the collateral or "secondary" objective of proving that wars of national liberation are "not an easy way, a cheap way, for the expansion of communism in the future."

Are these mere semantic differences or are there important implications that flow from the difference between causing an opponent to desist and defeating one's opponent? Yes, there is a fundamental difference between the forces needed and the methods employed to attempt to cause the enemy to desist from doing unwanted acts and the forces needed and methods employed when one intends to defeat the enemy by destroying him.

The United States was at pains to point out to the North Vietnamese leadership that the United States did not intend to overthrow the Hanoi regime. That being the case, it had to be the intention of the United States to modify the behavior of the Hanoi Politburo with respect to its neighbor to the South. Such a goal, although probably absolutely fascinating to the psychologist, was probably unattainable. As diplomat and historian George Kennan said about World War I and II:

> Both wars were fought, really, with a view to changing Germany: to correcting her behavior, to making the Germans something different from what they were. Yet, there is no evidence that the post–World War II Germans are any different. Germany ceased to be a military threat to either East or West because, by 1945, Germany was cut in half. This political surgery has simply foreclosed her ability to act in ways which are internationally antisocial. Hitler was unreconstructed to the bitter end. The Nazi leadership was not modified, it was replaced by political figures, such as [Konrad] Adenauer, who had possessed a different Weltanschauung all along, but who could not or would not seize the levers of power from the National Socialists. To replace Hitler required a German defeat. Thus, altering a nation's actions flows as a consequence of that nation's military defeat rather than from an abstraction such as modifying the behavior of its ruling elite.

However, in 1965, United States grand strategy was to cause the enemy to desist, and thus, either the Joint Chiefs of Staff or General Westmoreland would have to develop a military strategy which would achieve the policy aims of the government and yet make military sense to the soldiers who would have to carry out those orders. It is at this point that Dr. Amos A. Jordan faults the Joint Chiefs of Staff for not being more effective in translating United States aims from the macro-scale as seen by Washington to the micro-scale that needed to be understood by the commanders in the field, and conversely, for not being able to demonstrate convincingly to the secretary of defense and the commander-in-chief that the aims, as stated, were not capable of attainment within the constraints imposed by the Johnson Administration.

Were the policy aims of the United States in Vietnam such to enhance the success of the military strategy? This question cannot be answered in isolation. In order to determine the answer, it is necessary to examine, at the same time, the answer to the next question: *Was the military strategy the correct one to accomplish the aims of policy?*

Hopefully, such a tangle would not exist. Ideally, the aims of policy would be stated in clear, unambiguous language. Who would expect that the United States would take as its aim the behavior modification of the ruling elite of a small Asian half-nation on the border of Communist China? But it did, and it can be argued that such an unusual aim would be very difficult to attain by military means short of destruction or overthrow of the rulers of the opposing country. And yet, it was also the aim of the United States not to destroy or overthrow the Hanoi government. Indeed, the military strategy that could accomplish the aim of United States policy would have to be extraordinarily brilliant and would have to be given an almost unlimited time to accomplish such a task.

But former Secretary of State Dean Rusk made a strong case that we had every reason to believe we could induce the North Vietnamese to desist in the South:

> Bear in mind that in this post-war period, the democracies, primarily in the United States, have felt that there were times when it was necessary to take action which would deny to the aggressor his targets without plunging the world into World War III. For example, we managed to "winkle" the Soviet forces out of Iran by action in the UN Security Council. We managed to give enough aid to the Greeks so that we won that one within Greece. In the case of Berlin, instead of going to war with the Soviet Union, when they blockaded Berlin, we used an airlift for several months to get some time to try to work it out by diplomatic means and we were successful in that. In the case of Korea, President Truman wasn't about to get us involved in a general war with China—several hundred million people over there—but tried to preserve the status quo ante without a general war. So that same combination of resistance plus restraint was also part of our approach to Vietnam. But this was not unique to Vietnam. It has been characteristic of all post-war foreign policy. You see if you just turn your back on some of these problems for five minutes, you can have World War III. And those that realize what World War III means realize that you must not turn your back and let that happen.

Wearing Down the Enemy

The military strategy devised by General Westmoreland and his staff was called "attrition." The beauty of the attrition strategy was that it appeared to answer the expectations of those who merely wanted to cause the enemy to desist and it met the expectations of those who felt the enemy would have to be defeated.

Basically, attrition envisioned causing the enemy to use up his supplies and manpower at a higher rate than he could replace them. Ultimately, so the theory went, the enemy would run out of supplies and troops and thus would no longer be able to torment the GVN. This gave the United States ground troops the mission to seek out the enemy, to destroy him if contacted and failing that, to at least keep him on the move expending his supplies without recourse to his accustomed caches and expending his energy as well while struggling to avoid the United States troops.

Apparently, the decision-makers failed to realize that the enemy need only move back into the sanctuaries of Cambodia or Laos to lick its wounds, to rest, and be resupplied. The folly of sanctuary warfare would manifest itself time and time again. Thus, the decision-makers' fear of creating a wider war, doomed the strategy of attrition to failure.

Unfortunately, General Westmoreland's military strategy was based upon assumptions about the means that would be allotted to support his strategy and about the conditions under which the strategy would be undertaken, which did not prove true. Added to that handicap was the far from perfect knowledge the United States had about North Vietnamese capabilities and Sino-Soviet intentions. Westmoreland assumed that he would eventually be given the strength to isolate the battlefield and that the makers of grand strategy would allow the military the necessary freedom of action to defeat the enemy in South Vietnam. Dean Rusk admits that a major error in United States Vietnam policy was to underestimate the staying power of the North Vietnamese. In addition, the United States could never be certain what United States actions might provoke a more active role by the Russians or the Red Chinese.

Attrition depended, in part, upon being able to maintain the pressure on the enemy but when the enemy did not wish to give battle it was extremely difficult to find him. For example, after the first Battle of the Ia Drang in October–November 1965, the NVA pulled back into Cambodia west of Duc Co and would not give battle. The same process occurred in October 1966 after the Second Battle of the Ia Drang. Operation Paul Revere IV, designed to retain contact with the NVA, produced almost no enemy contacts after the NVA retreated to its Cambodian sanctuaries. If the enemy could not be brought to combat, he could not be forced to expend his ammunition.

IV. A War in Search of Strategy

A major flaw in the attrition strategy attempted within the confines of South Vietnam was that it actually gave the initiative to the North Vietnamese. They, thanks to the terrain, vegetation, and the luxury of almost inviolable sanctuaries, could determine the level of the intensity of combat. Thus, the level of casualties and supply expenditure became not a function of the decision-makers in Washington or the military strategists in Saigon, but crucial factors determined in Hanoi. Moreover, fear of Soviet or Chinese intervention meant that U.S. strategy was, in part, being dictated from Moscow and Beijing.

If necessary, the NVA/VC could live off the land or take advantage of the VC infrastructure before it became almost moribund. Moreover, a corrupt government official could be found now and again who would let GVN supplies get into the hands of the NVA/VC. Intimidation was sometimes as effective as corruption. The all-too-often under-armed and undertrained Popular Force Platoons were often unfairly maligned, but it is true that some of them would leave a box of ammunition outside their defenses just before nightfall in order to buy another night without a NVA/VC attack.

Also, not enough importance had been attached to demographics. As it turned out, the North Vietnamese population was large enough to produce enough persons of military age to maintain a significant presence in South Vietnam indefinitely. This was so even after subtracting the often highly inflated body counts reported by the ARVN and the only slightly less inflated body counts turned in by a few, but by no means all, United States units. Thomas C. Thayer, in *The Lessons of Vietnam*, said:

> By the middle of 1967 it was clear that the availability of North Vietnamese manpower and the willingness to send it South would prevent the allies from winning the war of attrition. After more than two years of American troop involvement, the number of NVA troops in South Vietnam was less than two percent of the North Vietnamese male labor force, less than three percent of the male agricultural force. By comparison, the U.S. forces in Southeast Asia at that time amounted to about one percent of our male civilian labor force.

Finally, attrition is only a viable military strategy when, in addition to forcing consumption of supplies on hand, one can cut off the possibility of resupply. According to Thomas C. Thayer, "there were plenty of supplies to ship, because the estimated flow of imports into North Vietnam was twenty times the size of estimated supply shipments from North Vietnam into Laos." The failure of the United States to seal North Vietnam off from its sources of supply made the task of the air interdiction campaign not only impossible, but endless. The task was made even more difficult by the policy of gradual application of airpower in the early stages of the air war and by the detailed control of individual airstrikes by McNamara and Johnson.

By the time the air commanders in the field regained control of their operations, the bombing began to experience a series of politically inspired pauses and halts. Even so, the air interdiction campaign managed to destroy about two-thirds of the supplies the North Vietnamese tried to send overland into South Vietnam. However, what did get through was enough to keep the NVA/VC in the war because about 70 percent of what the NVA/VC needed to continue operations in South Vietnam came from sources inside the country. The ability to vary the intensity of their effort allowed the NVA/VC to remain viable. When supplies became too few, they simply reduced the scale of their operations.

Thus, without the effective isolation of the battlefield and without forcing the enemy to consume his supplies and manpower at a rate faster than they could be replaced, attrition would have to fail and some other means of forcing the enemy to desist would have to be found. Unfortunately, it would be some time before it was recognized by the framers of the grand strategy that the aim of causing the enemy to desist was illusory and that time would become the ally of the North Vietnamese rather than the Americans.

As pressure mounted upon the administration in Washington to wind down American involvement in Vietnam, it became clear that an American solution would have to be found quickly or the war would have to be turned over to someone else. Thus, the war would have to either be fully Americanized or fully Vietnamized.

Americanization vs. Vietnamization— The Phan Thiet Experiment

Perhaps what was needed was more Americanization earlier and more Vietnamization later. In the Korean War, the United States adhered to the principle of Unity of Command through the device of the United Nations Command and in the person of one supreme commander over all military forces and all civilian agencies within the combat zone.

Unity of Command was acceptable to all parties concerned in Korea because the aggression was so naked and so serious that there was no time to worry about questions of sovereignty and bureaucratic prerogatives. In Vietnam, however, the aggressors were careful to carry the theme of homegrown revolution throughout the war even though as early as 1965, it became necessary to introduce regular NVA formations into South Vietnam. Moreover, even after Tet 1968, when the war effort fell almost exclusively upon the NVA, the North Vietnamese were careful to insist upon the homegrown revolution façade.

What would have been the result had a Korean War type command been established prior to the time that United States public support for the war became eroded? To say that it was not attempted and thus we will never know is not quite accurate. It was attempted in a portion of the province of Binh Thuan.

In the fall of 1966, a battalion task force (2nd Battalion, 7th Cavalry) from the 1st Air Cavalry Division was formed under the command of Lt. Colonel Billy Vaughn and placed in Binh Thuan Province with its headquarters in the provincial capital of Phan Thiet. The battalion fought several successful engagements against the VC. Shortly after Colonel Vaughn completed his time in command, Lieutenant General Stanley R. Larsen, the United States II Field Force Commander, was able to negotiate a unique command arrangement between the United States forces in the area and Lt. Colonel De, the Vietnamese district chief. The arrangement made the commander of the 2nd Battalion, 7th Cavalry the virtual warlord of the area. The fortunate beneficiary of this arrangement was the new battalion commander, Lt. Colonel Fred E. Karhohs.

Colonel Karhohs, with the reins of power over all military forces and civilian agencies in his hands, was able to turn an already successful military operation into a spectacular military and civilian triumph. In addition to having absolute control of the human resources in the area, Colonel Karhohs reduced daytime military operations and took the night away from the enemy by an aggressive program of night ambushes. Soon, the entire area was secure and the work of the Civil Operations and Rural Development Support teams (CORDS) went forward.

The Phan Thiet operation became a showcase for the principle of Unity of Command. Almost every senior United States official to visit Vietnam was taken to be briefed at Phan Thiet. Unfortunately, the concept could never be sold to the decision-makers in Washington and Saigon. The other misfortune of Phan Thiet was that visitors could easily get the impression that the war was being won countrywide when, in fact, Phan Thiet was an anomaly resting upon a unique command arrangement.

The war was being won in Phan Thiet. In fact, it was over. Behind the security screen of the 2nd Battalion, 7th Cavalry and the Vietnamese units under its control, the GVN began the erection of a government responsive to the needs of the district and which, under the watchful eyes of Colonel Karhohs and his successors, actually delivered what it promised.

Looking back, Karhohs, one of the Army's youngest major generals who retired to become president of a successful corporation, said,

> One could call this concept Americanization. It was a very successful operation in that we were able to control a significant enemy force with a relatively small but highly mobile military force, to include South Vietnamese Army elements with a unified command arrangement that gives the U.S. commander complete tactical control over all friendly elements in his sector of operation.

Phan Thiet received a heavy VC attack at Tet 1968, but did not rally to the side of the VC. Nor was there a civilian uprising during the debacle of 1975 when South Vietnam collapsed. Phan Thiet was, in due course, simply overrun by the NVA tide as it swept southward down the coast—the end of an experiment in Americanization that might have led to the truly effective Vietnamization of both the political and military effort.

Another way of reducing the human cost to the United States would have been to have gotten more of the nations in the region involved in the fighting. However, the fears of the United States about the communist threat to South Vietnam did not have the same importance to many living nearer the threat than did the United States. Nevertheless, the United States was able to interest an ally already facing a serious communist threat to her own borders to send some first-rate troops.

The South Koreans

The Republic of Korea deployed two and a half divisions of its Army in South Vietnam. Unfortunately, they were not used as fully as they could have been. The ROK forces were hard, tough, well-trained soldiers, but instead of employing them in the unpopulated border regions to assist in the fight against the NVA invasion, they were given Tactical Areas of Responsibility (TAOR) in the highly populated coastal provinces.

The ROK divisions were highly effective in pacifying the static areas they occupied, but they were effective in a cold, hard way. They clamped an iron, uncompromising hand upon their areas that snuffed out the activities of the NVA/VC, but also seemed to cast a chill over all aspects of

Vietnamese life. Their areas were peaceful in time, but peaceful in the way that the streets of East Berlin were peaceful—somewhat like a beehive to which the beekeeper has applied an overdose of smoke.

The South Korean contribution, nevertheless, was valuable. But it would have been most interesting to have seen what the ROKs would have done against the NVA along the DMZ or along the Laotian and Cambodian borders. No doubt their casualties would have been higher. It may have been that the ROK government had specified that the ROK forces would only be used in the Maritime provinces. After all, the ROK faced, and still does, a major communist threat to its own existence and that could be reason enough to put a limit upon the scope of their operations and to keep them in position for prompt withdrawal, if needed at home.

In fact, the ROKS were never under the command of General Westmoreland. Their activities were coordinated through a Free World Forces Council composed of COMUSMACV, the commander of the ROK forces in South Vietnam and the chairman of the Vietnamese Joint General Staff. War by committee, however amiable, was just another handicap imposed upon General Westmoreland—a commander who was trying to make the best of an incoherent grand strategy.

The Hourglass War

The contradictions between the grand strategy of desist and the military strategy of defeat resulted in a war of attrition which was fatally handicapped by confining General Westmoreland's area of operations to the territory of South Vietnam and by providing him only enough forces to react to each new threat raised by the enemy *inside* South Vietnam. Thus, the Vietnam War was fought in the dimension of time rather than space. The outcome became dependent upon which side had the greater amount of time at its disposal. Because the totalitarian regimes are not as sensitive to public opinion as are democratic governments, the time dimension provided the North Vietnamese a significant advantage in dealing with its much more powerful adversary. General Westmoreland was aware of this problem:

> By the time we had enough forces to attempt to physically cut off the infiltration through Laos and from North Vietnam, the Johnson Administration was so intimidated by the dissenters that it had no heart for it. Privately, General Wheeler and I hoped for a new Administration that would allow us to get the war over with,

but when the public was led to misperceive what Tet 1968 really meant we lost all chance of cutting the NVA off from its sources of men and supplies.

Were adequate means allotted to support the strategy? In a strict sense the answer would be, no. If the grand strategy did not allow for an invasion of North Vietnam to defeat the aggression at its source, then the 550,000 troops eventually allotted to General Westmoreland were insufficient to deal with the Viet Cong, to chase the North Vietnamese Army in South Vietnam, to form a barrier along the DMZ, and to cut the infiltration routes through Laos. Estimates by the Army chief of staff in 1965 called for one United States division for security in South Vietnam and four U.S./SEATO divisions to provide a barrier against infiltration. This, of course, was in addition to the armed forces of South Vietnam.

At the height of the war, the Free World Forces had the equivalent of 12 divisions inside Vietnam and still had insufficient force to put the four division anti-infiltration barrier in place. If 12 divisions could not cause the enemy to desist in his efforts against the South Vietnamese, one would think the grand strategy of desist was incapable of accomplishment by the military strategy of attrition. At some point, it should have become obvious that United States aims in Vietnam could not be accomplished unless the grand strategy was changed to one of defeating the enemy.

In the classic sense, an enemy is defeated by destroying his ability to make war. Historian Russell Weigley argues that when the United States has possessed the strength to do so, this has been the approach it has taken to war: "In the Indian wars, the Civil War, and then climactically in World War II, American strategists sought in actuality the object that Clausewitz saw as that of the ideal type of war, of war in the abstract: 'the destruction of the enemy's armed forces, amongst all the objects which can be pursued in War, appears always as the one which overrules all others.'"

Not even the Korean War experience caused the Army's multilevel system of branch, command and staff, and senior service colleges to stop teaching the desirability of "victory" and the necessity of destroying the enemy's ability to fight. Thus, the military officer is conditioned to strike right at the heart of the matter—to destroy the enemy's armed forces, to annihilate them because that is seen as the quickest and least costly way (in terms of men and treasure) of bringing the entire unpleasant business to a speedy end. George Kennan, in *American Diplomacy,* captured the essence of this spirit when he wrote that

[A] democracy is peace-loving. It does not like to go to war. It is slow to rise to provocation. When it has once been provoked to the point where it must grasp the sword it does not easily forgive its adversary for having produced this situation. Democracy fights in anger—it fights to punish the power that was rash enough and hostile enough to provoke it—to teach that power a lesson it will not forget, to prevent the thing from happening again. Such a war must be carried to the bitter end.

If so, how could the United States have destroyed its opponents in Vietnam? To do that would have required adequate means operating under favorable conditions.

First, the North Vietnamese Army would have to be brought to battle. Yet, with 550,000 United States troops at his command, General Westmoreland was unable to get the North Vietnamese Army to fight unless it chose to do so. The simple answer is that the Free World Forces would have to threaten something so vital to the North Vietnamese armed forces that they would have to give battle. Certainly, there was nothing inside the territory of South Vietnam that was so meaningful to the NVA that they would engage in climactic battle. Therefore, an invasion of North Vietnam with the capability, but not necessarily the intention of *destroying* the North Vietnamese state would have forced the issue.

At that point, the capabilities and intentions of Communist China would have to be considered. Would the destruction of the Armed Forces of North Vietnam been worth the risk of a wider war which would have pitted the United States against Communist China? Also, what would be the Soviet reaction to the snuffing out of the military life of North Vietnam? Could the communist world have tolerated the humiliation of the defeat of North Vietnam? Since the United States did not take this course of action, we shall never know, but the Sino-Soviet reaction was of paramount concern to the framers of American grand strategy. Again, we see the folly of fighting a war in which major elements of strategy are dictated by hostile nation-states.

The pity is that those charged with the formulation of grand strategy either never thought all of this through or never gave enough credence to intelligence reports on the enemy's capabilities. As to the home front, the planners discounted the results of war games foretelling of Americans rioting in the streets to protest the continuation of the war. With perfect hindsight, it is easy to say what might have been, but if President Johnson had had more capacity in foreign affairs, he might have limited the American effort to providing aid and advice and allowed the politics of Southeast Asia to reach whatever conclusions the Southeast Asians could reach among themselves.

But the United States, in its time, could not resist the whirlpool tug of the forces set in motion with the end of the colonial era. Once caught in the undertow, the United States, search as it might, did not find a strategy to end the war within the constraints of the Sino-Soviet threat and within the patience of its people to whom the American stake, vital or peripheral, was unclear.

The search for a winning strategy was almost as troubled as it was unsuccessful, but the trouble was not just in Vietnam. On the banks of the Potomac, a contest was fought that produced its own casualties. Its victims varied: reputations, careers, and the fortunes of a political party, but its chief casualty was the outcome of the American effort in Southeast Asia.

V

Riverine Warfare— On the Potomac

Lenin said long ago that the road to victory in Asia passed through Paris and London. In this case [Vietnam], the road passed through Washington.
—Major General Adrian St. John II

In writing about a war, there is the temptation to focus upon the actual fighting, but there are actually other battles that may have more to do with the outcome of the war than what men do with rifles and bombs. These are the battles fought, not in the mud, but around conference tables and in the briefing rooms where decisions are made. For it is in these settings that important battles are fought—the battles that determine what *means* will be available to the commanders in the field and the *conditions* under which they will be allowed to use those means.

The Point of Decision

The importance of the commander being at the point of decision is one of the eternal verities drummed into the heads of officer-students in the United States Army's extensive school system. Simply put, this dictum states that it is crucial for the commander to be at the right place on the battlefield at the right time and by his leadership to influence the action. At the tactical level in South Vietnam, this age-old truism was proven again and again. Indeed, due to the helicopter and the radio, there were times when too many commanders assembled at (or more often above) the decisive point on the battlefield. Sometimes, this was a blessing to those facing the enemy on the ground and sometimes it was not. Nevertheless, the point about the importance of the decisive place on the battlefield is made.

General Westmoreland, the officer responsible for the war inside of

61

South Vietnam, could not be at the decisive point to influence the outcome of his military strategy of attrition. The decisive point was not in South Vietnam. It was in Washington, D.C.

To examine this assertion one can turn once again to the model relationship described in previous chapters and consider the last two questions that can be extrapolated from the model:

1. Were adequate means allotted to support the strategy?
2. Was the strategy undertaken under favorable circumstances?

The answers to these two questions cannot be found in South Vietnam because the means allotted to accomplish the military strategy of attrition and the circumstances under which the strategy was undertaken were decided along the Potomac and not along the Mekong River in Vietnam.

For the attrition strategy to have been successful, it would have been necessary to isolate the battlefield and to have the means to hound the NVA/VC to exhaustion and/or bring them to give climactic battle. If the NVA/VC could not be cut off from their sources of manpower, supply, and direction, the war in South Vietnam could only become a protracted struggle, the outcome of which would depend upon which side had the greater will to prevail.

Thus, to understand how the American military could be so successful in the vast majority of its contacts with the enemy in South Vietnam and for the war to still be lost, the prosecution of the overall war effort in Southeast Asia must be examined in the context of the struggle taking place within the Johnson Administration and in the context of the American public's understanding of the nature and progress of the war.

Isolation of the Battlefield

Attempts have been made to compare the war in South Vietnam with the British experience in putting down the communist insurgency in Malaya. Although there were, of course, several dissimilarities in the two situations, it should be noted that the British were able to cut the Malaysian peninsula off from the sources of communist manpower and supplies. Sir Robert Thompson, the architect of the British victory, said, "If it [South Vietnam] had been surrounded by sea, except on the DMZ (as in South Korea) there would have been no problem at all; the war would have been won years ago and the North could have been held at bay indefinitely."

V. Riverine Warfare—On the Potomac

Whether the United States could have isolated South Vietnam may be a moot question at that stage, but it must be said that the framers of grand strategy in Washington during the Johnson Administration would not permit the American military to carry out the operations necessary to effect the isolation of the battlefield in South Vietnam. Effective isolation would have required a concert of air, sea and ground operations; however, in practice, each type of operation was either attempted alone or in concert with only one of the other modalities and/or attempted in insufficient force to be effective.

For example, MARKET TIME, the joint United States–South Vietnamese campaign to prevent the infiltration of men and supplies from entering South Vietnam by sea, was a smashing success. However, neither MARKET TIME nor any other naval operation attempted to prevent the flow of communist war material from entering the North Vietnamese port of Haiphong or the Cambodian port of Sihanoukville.

On the ground, General Westmoreland was prohibited from attacking the communist sanctuaries in Cambodia or from cutting the Laotian corridor through which the NVA infiltrated into South Vietnam or into Cambodia and thence into South Vietnam. In addition to the politically imposed prohibition upon such operations, there was also the fact that General Westmoreland was never given sufficient troops to secure the South Vietnam homeland and, at the same time, to erect a troop barrier in the north against foot infiltration.

The air interdiction campaign, in order to contribute its full measure to the isolation effect, should have been conducted with maximum shock effect upon all war targets and activities in North Vietnam, Laos, and Cambodia. In practice, it was executed in a halting, tentative manner explained by a variety of rationales—all of which might have been correct in their season.

Sometimes, the bombing outside of South Vietnam was explained as "tit for tat" reprisals, as an attempt at air interdiction, as a means of raising the price of aggression, as a bargaining chip in negotiations, and finally, in the Nixon Administration, as the only means left to pound the North Vietnamese to engage in meaningful negotiations in Paris and to force the return of the American POWs.

As seen in the context of World War II and the Korean War, total air interdiction is not possible except under the most favorable geographic circumstances. Certainly, the geography of Southeast Asia made the air task exceedingly difficult and, when compounded by the political restraints and the civilian controls imposed by Washington, total air interdiction became an expensive exercise in frustration with severe political liabilities at home and abroad.

Paradoxically, the decision to bomb North Vietnam and the control of that bombing were major preoccupations of the civilian hierarchy in Washington, whereas the decision to put ground troops ashore was made with a comparative lack of concern and deliberation. Another paradox is that although the United States Air Force, United States Navy, and the Marines deployed in Southeast Asia had the most powerful and sophisticated air armadas ever assembled, the end result of their use was the most indecisive in our history, albeit not the fault of the pilots who flew the missions.

Civilian Command and Control

One of the most striking features of the Vietnam War was the degree to which civilian officials dictated not only what military actions were to be undertaken but also how they were to be conducted. The best example of this phenomenon can be found in the air operations conducted in North Vietnam and in the Laotian corridor.

The problem began when the Joint Chiefs of Staff responded to a request from Secretary McNamara to provide a list of what they felt to be the most important airstrike targets in North Vietnam. In turn, CINCPAC selected a list of 94 targets that were included in a plan for an air campaign against North Vietnam. This plan was approved by the Joint Chiefs of Staff on April 17, 1964; however, Joint Chiefs of Staff approval was to have little bearing on how the plan was executed.

At first, United States air attacks were limited to reprisals. Initially, in August 1964, attacks were made against enemy torpedo boats, their docks, and fuel storage facilities in reprisal for attacks by North Vietnamese patrol boats against United States destroyers operating in the Gulf of Tonkin. While reprisal became the rationale for the Gulf of Tonkin Resolution that granted almost unlimited war powers to President Johnson, a growing body of evidence suggests that actual North Vietnamese attacks on U.S. destroyers never took place. Nevertheless, following the alleged incidents in the Gulf of Tonkin, U.S. air attacks were increased on a tit for tat basis related to mortar and ground attacks launched by the VC against United States installations in South Vietnam. On February 13, 1965,

President Johnson made the decision to inaugurate a sustained, but in many ways limited, air campaign against North Vietnam. This program bore the code name "Rolling Thunder."

In accordance with the United States Air Force doctrine, the first steps in an air campaign should include the establishment of air superiority over the area of operations and the elimination or suppression of the enemy's air defense capabilities. Then, having rendered the enemy incapable of defense against air attack, attacks against strategic targets, i.e., those giving the enemy the capability to wage war, could be carried out quickly and effectively with little or no losses to the attacking force. Unfortunately for the United States Air Force and United States Navy aircrews sent to attack North Vietnam, President Johnson and his civilian advisers would allow political and psychological considerations to outweigh the proven military approach to air operations. As General Theodore R. Milton, USAF, who was a major general on the CINCPAC staff recalled, "The initial series of Rolling Thunder air strikes were both political and psychological in nature. Target selection, forces, munitions used, and even the timing of the strikes were decided in Washington. Targets struck were barracks, radar sites, ammunition depots, and military vehicles—all in the southernmost part of North Vietnam."

Initially, nothing was done to eliminate the fleet of MiG interceptors which the North Vietnamese had sitting at various airbases or to begin the comprehensive elimination of North Vietnamese anti-aircraft defenses. Ironically, this failure to follow the classic set of task priorities would allow the North Vietnamese time to improve their anti-air defenses resulting in a needlessly higher loss rate, and gave the North Vietnamese a large number of United States airmen as hostages to use against the United States in subsequent diplomatic contacts and negotiations.

The list of 94 targets was not used by President Johnson as a description of the targets to be eliminated in a comprehensive air campaign; instead, it was used as a shopping list from which the president and his civilian advisers would pick and choose according to their fancy and according to what they thought would transmit just the right signal to Hanoi. General Milton recounted:

> The people in the Johnson Administration had some interesting ideas about transmitting signals to Hanoi. One day they would OK a target to the East of Hanoi and then the next day they would OK one to the West of Hanoi. Then they would follow that with permission for us to strike a target to the North and one to the South of Hanoi. They didn't seem to care much about the nature of the target other than

the concern we all shared to avoid civilian casualties. I suppose the idea was to scare Hanoi with a demonstration that we had the ability to strike all around their capital city.

The Joint Chiefs of Staff pressed for an all-out campaign if the North Vietnamese lines of communication were to be interdicted. According to *The Tale of Two Bridges and the Battle for the Skies Over North Vietnam,* edited by Major A. J. C. Lavalle, "the Joint Chiefs and Air Force Chief of Staff General McConnell in particular, believed the most successful interdiction strategy would be one of short duration and broad scope. General McConnell argued for a 28-day air campaign in which all of the 94 targets on the JCS list would be destroyed, including those around Hanoi." However, the Joint Chiefs of Staff as a body opted for a 12-week program "intended to isolate North Vietnam from all external sources of resupply, and then to destroy her internal military and industrial capacity." But, not even the 12-week plan was put into effect.

As time went on, Secretary McNamara decided the airstrikes were not going to produce the results he wanted, either in controlling the flow of communist men and supplies to the south or in forcing the North Vietnamese to desist in their efforts to reunite Vietnam by force. Moreover, Ambassador Taylor in Saigon was becoming annoyed with the lack of purpose and firmness indicated by the halting nature of the airstrikes and began to complain to Washington. Slowly, Mr. McNamara began to allow the commanders on the scene to have a little more latitude in target selection, but he still kept unprecedented rein upon the air war.

At the outset, if a target was not on the approved list, CINCPAC could not even ask to strike it. It had to be placed on the list first. This made targets of opportunity, such as military truck convoys headed toward South Vietnam, off-limits. The aircrews could only grit their teeth as they watched the NVA moving into South Vietnam and Laos.

On one of McNamara's trips to visit CINCPAC in Hawaii, General Milton pressed the secretary for permission to conduct armed reconnaissance along the roads in the southern panhandle region of North Vietnam. McNamara asked what was meant by "armed reconnaissance." General Milton explained to him that armed reconnaissance was merely the reconnaissance of a prescribed area by armed aircraft that were free to engage proper military targets of opportunity. Reluctantly, McNamara agreed but, still unwilling to lose control of even this limited facet of the air war, restricted the number of sorties to 25 per week. General Milton objected to this because he saw no advantage in this restriction and many disadvantages.

For example, the 25 sorties would have to be divided between the United States Air Force, the United States Navy and the Marines because each service had valid requirements for such missions. By the time the sorties were divided each squadron would get only four or less sorties per week. If two aircraft were sent out on armed reconnaissance, only two sorties were left for the week. There would be a natural and prudent desire to husband the remaining sorties to have a reserve of armed reconnaissance. If bad weather then came in and prevented the two remaining sorties from being flown, they were lost forever because McNamara did not permit them to be carried over to the next week. Then too, higher priority missions might be assigned to the squadron's aircraft and by the time they got around to flying the armed reconnaissance sorties the weather might not permit their accomplishment. Thus, the restriction mitigated against the 25 sorties ever being flown in one week.

On McNamara's next trip to CINCPAC, General Milton asked that the restriction on armed reconnaissance sorties be lifted. The secretary immediately flipped to a page in his ever-present notebook of facts and said, "You see I've got you! Look here, three weeks ago you only used 18 sorties and the week after that only 12 and last week it was 16. Now why should I give you more armed reconnaissance sorties?"

What is remarkable about all of this is not the picture of an Air Force general having to explain the intricacies of squadron operations in order to get enough freedom of action to make the system work, but the fact that the secretary of defense, with all of his enormous responsibilities for the conduct of the defense establishment worldwide, would involve himself in this level of detail.

As General Westmoreland said in a speech, "The trouble was that our bombing was off and on—a thermometer of political pressure at home. Hanoi had time to adjust itself to every escalatory step.... The control and prosecution of the war was not conducive to conducting it." Based on President Kennedy's tight control of tactical military action during the Cuban Missile Crisis, the Kennedy Administration advisers whom President Johnson retained saw such control as the modern way to confront an enemy. Allegedly, President Johnson once boasted, "My boys can't even bomb an outhouse without my approval."

But the issue of tight personal civilian control over military operations went deeper than just the Cuban Missile Crisis. It rested, as John B. Keeley pointed out so well, upon the computer and communications revolutions:

Formula for Failure in Vietnam

Military organizations are decision-making hierarchies. The combat organization of the Army and Marine Corps, for example, dates back to the 18th Century. Companies, battalions, regiments, brigades, divisions and corps are organizations whose origins stem from the requirement to organize the command structure to meet the demands of battlefields vastly different from those of today....

These organizations reflected a balance between authority and responsibility. The size and function of each level of organization was such that it could be commanded. With responsibility defined in such a way, authority could be divided accordingly. Thus, this balance between authority and responsibility was, easily understood and facilitated the conduct of operations....

It is generally understood that the nature of the battlefield and command and control have been dramatically altered by technology.... Less well understood is that the balance between authority and responsibility has been gravely disturbed at almost all levels of organization by this new information technology. One need only recall Admiral Anderson's confrontation with Mr. McNamara in the Navy's flag plot over the location of ships during the Cuba Blockade, or the layering of command and control helicopters above company fire fights in Vietnam to appreciate the blurring of the traditional concepts of authority and responsibility that has occurred because of modern communications.

To the discomfort of the military, the computer and communications revolutions coincided with the arrival of a secretary of defense who was a true believer in the application of the new technologies to management problems. A major general, who, as a lieutenant colonel, served on a ballistic missile study team that reported directly to McNamara, observed:

McNamara had many good ideas. He brought a lot of sound disciplined management techniques that had not existed before to the Military Departments. However, I would have to judge him, over all, as a mediocre SECDEF. He placed an unrealistically high reliance on ORSA techniques to solve problems or define decision options. He failed to recognize, or chose to ignore, the simple truth that many important, and perhaps decisive, factors in the military equation defy analytical quantification; e.g., morale, command and control, motivation, the confusion of battle, etc. He tended to reject recommendations based primarily on military judgment and military experience.

Presumably, raising the level at which decisions are made would tend to make war more impersonal and thus it would become easier for those far removed from the battlefield to give orders that eventually result in killing and maiming. But, in the case of Robert McNamara, there is evidence that this was not so. For example, Paul Nitze, who served under McNamara, contends the secretary of defense was painfully aware of the death-dealing consequences of each air sortie he authorized:

McNamara was deeply affected by reading the manuscript of a series of articles later published in *The New Yorker* and as a book, *The Village of Ben Sue*. The author, Jonathan Schell, came into McNamara's office and briefed him on what he had seen in Vietnam. He said that he had been asked by *The New Yorker* to write a series of articles on the subject. McNamara put him in the next office, gave him a secretary, and said, "Write it. I want to read it." He read the draft before it was even submitted to *The New Yorker*. He was horrified by its stories of meaningless and random bombings by our air force, by the cynical attitude toward human life which, it purported, permeated our forces. He circulated a draft in the Pentagon and to the commanders in Vietnam and asked for comments on what was wrong with it. Obviously, there were things wrong with it; it wasn't wholly accurate. But still the essence of it appeared to be valid. I think this brought him to the realization that we had not been fighting the war correctly; we were using firepower too indiscriminately, with insufficient discipline and in a manner which was often counterproductive.

As it wore on, McNamara became increasingly melancholy about the war and especially the bombing. Indeed, there was perhaps a measure of Hamlet in McNamara. If there had been in him less Hamlet and more Clausewitz, McNamara might have been better able to understand the views of the professional military who were arguing that the path to less suffering and destruction was clearly posted by such principles of war as: Objective, Offensive, Mass, Unity of Command and Surprise. Henry L. Trewhitt, in his book *McNamara*, points up this facet of Secretary McNamara's personality:

> While he agreed with the American purpose and advised the use of force, he had no stomach for the fighting as the bloodshed increased. "He recognized and pursued the requirement for military power," a respected senior general observed. It was a great practical and intellectual challenge. Still, he was reluctant to use it as it had to be used. I had to tell him, "Mr. Secretary, it is sometimes necessary to use force for the greater good of the nation."

Mr. McNamara, despite his reluctance to use military power as an instrument of violence, understood power very well. He knew that no matter how many memoranda the Joint Chiefs of Staff wrote trying to gain support for a "win the war" grand strategy, the Joint Chiefs of Staff were virtually powerless. It was McNamara who controlled the strength levels, and it was McNamara who controlled the budget. Thus, it was not until November 11, 1966 (20 months after the first United States forces went ashore in South Vietnam), that McNamara even bothered to reply to the attempts by the Joint Chiefs of Staff to get the strategy issue resolved. It was not fair of Mr. McNamara to do that, commented General Westmoreland. He continued, "He told me many times to ask for what I needed to do what they wanted me to do and not to worry about the political, psychological or economic aspects. He said he would take care of that and if my requests became intolerable, he would have to make a decision. But, when I put in my requests, McNamara invariably cut them back."

Ironically, the result of irresolution, hesitancy, diffusion of effort, vacillation, and compromise was the largest bomb tonnage ever dropped in any war and, at the time, the longest and most costly war in American history. All the military criticisms of McNamara were incorporated in the remark of a senior commander: "He gave us enough to deny success to the enemy. He did not give us enough to make the enemy stop trying." In another irony, McNamara, the man with great sympathy for the unfortunates in the war zone, was a man of iron will in dealing with those whose task it was to conduct the war. General William E. DePuy, who served both in Vietnam and in the Pentagon during the McNamara years, said, "McNamara did intimidate the military more than most [all] other Sec/Defs. He was more arrogant—more cock-sure—tougher. He turned out also to be wrong—a bad combination."

Fred E. Karhohs, of Phan Thiet fame, who retired as a very young major general to launch an equally successful career as a corporation president, commented from his perspective as a member of the ISA under McNamara and a battalion and brigade commander in Vietnam:

> We erred from a strategic viewpoint in not applying more military pressure in several areas, with particular emphasis on North Vietnam. We took counsel of our fears and listened too often to the voices of doom and gloom. We allowed the enemy almost complete freedom of movement to the extent he rarely was required to keep active army forces at home. We allowed him to literally send every male of military age to fight in South Vietnam without fear of any "home-front" retaliation, except for highly "restricted" air raids.
>
> We followed a "civilian" strategy, one that was initially directed by Secretary McNamara and his principal civilian assistants, most of whom had little or no military experience. What was really needed in this time was another Harry Truman—someone who had the guts to mobilize the nation for an all-out effort. I know of no nice way to fight a war. Those individuals in the Pentagon and White House who came up with strategies of "surgical targeting," "selective raids," "graduated response," etc.—ad nauseam—simply never understood that there is no easy way to win a war. Our senior civilian leadership simply forgot all the lessons of history.
>
> The early military strategy for the Vietnam War was set in the large part by McNamara and his senior civilian advisors. We fought this war with one hand tied behind our back while taking on a very vicious enemy. Civilians, with little if any military experience, were actually directing, with varying degrees of specificity, military operational strategies to the Joint Chiefs of Staff. Had we fought World War II in this way, we would still be on the beaches of Normandy.

Paradoxically, while the Air Force and Navy were subject to the strictest and most detailed control from Washington over their operations outside of South Vietnam, General Westmoreland enjoyed little interference in the conduct of the ground war inside South Vietnam. With only a few exceptions, he was free to use his ground forces as he saw fit. His major handicaps, besides the lack of a grand strategy that could be converted to an accomplishable military strategy within South Vietnam, were insufficient forces and the fact that his charter as a commander did not encompass the entire war zone nor were all the forces operating inside South Vietnam under his command. It was only during the battle of Khe Sanh that all United States Air Force, Army, Navy, and Marine air assets were integrated into a command structure over which General Westmoreland had ultimate control. Khe Sanh was, of course, an exceptional situation in which the NVA massed two divisions in a two-month siege of 5,000 Marines. For a change, the NVA was concentrating on the battlefield around United States forces, making accurate intelligence on enemy locations easier to obtain.

With a unified intelligence gathering system directing the awesome power of the total air assets in Southeast Asia the NVA lost 20,000 troops killed-in-action versus Marine losses of 200. However, the enormity of the American victory should not bewitch one into attaching unwarranted significance to the outcome. Khe Sanh was an anomaly, just as Dien Bien Phu was an anomaly in the Indio-China War. Dien Bien Phu was significant because it erased public support in France for a continued French presence in Indo-China. The NVA defeat at the Khe Sanh had no such similar effect upon the North Vietnamese because their losses although appalling, were replaceable and the resolve of their leadership was apparently undiminished.

Had the United States failed to optimize its resources at Khe Sanh by placing them under a unified command, the outcome could have been considerably less spectacular. A kill ratio of 100:1 in any context is a victory but given the unrest and disillusion with the war in the United States, a kill ratio of something less could easily have been perceived as an American Dien Bien Phu. President Johnson was mindful of the political dangers of Khe Sanh and he repeatedly asked his military advisers for assurance that Khe Sanh would not turn into a Dien Bien Phu. General Westmoreland says President Johnson developed a fixation about Khe Sanh: "General Taylor had to set up a special White House Situation Room to depict and analyze American and enemy dispositions complete with a large aerial photograph and a terrain model." Johnson was fond of comparing himself with the "sad but steady" Abraham Lincoln and indeed both presidents shared a penchant for digging into the details of military operations. However, unlike Lincoln who could and did go and watch a battle in progress, Johnson, having spent only just over an hour at Cam Ranh Bay during the war, had to content himself with a terrain model.

Interference caused by Washington with General Westmoreland's operations seemed to be more concerned with the appearance of what Westmoreland was doing rather than with its substance. For example, in January 1966, the first United States Field Force under Lieutenant General Stanley R. "Swede" Larsen launched an operation called MASHER. Although the 42-day operation was a great success, before it was very far along President Johnson made it known that he did not like the name of the operation. To Johnson it implied that United States soldiers were "mashing" Asians. General Larsen, an officer widely cherished for a certain independence of thought, put his head together with Major General Harry W. O. Kinnard, the commander of the 1st Air Cavalry Division which was conducting the operation. They searched for the most pacifistic name they could imagine. The result: WHITE WING. That pacified the president, but to avoid tactical confusion, all subsequent operations orders used in the operation carried the double appellation: MASHER/WHITE WING. Most of the troops taking part were not aware of this background and presumably thought the cumbersome double name was the brainchild of some under-employed staff officer back in Nha Trang.

A more widely known example dealt with the term *search and destroy*. Its intended meaning was to describe a tactic by which small units would search for the NVA/VC and attempt to kill or capture them. In reality, search and destroy was just a flamboyant name for the time-honored tactic of "reconnaissance-in-force." But the press jumped on search and destroy as a prescription for United States troops to search everywhere and destroy everything and everyone on contact. Eventually, use of the term was forbidden and the use of "reconnaissance-in-force" was mandated.

In late 1966, General Westmoreland's headquarters directed that our Vietnamese allies were not to be referred to over the radio as "the little people." Such a term not only was deemed offensive to the diminutive Vietnamese, but also foolish as a communications security ploy. The directive went on to forbid the use of other terms such as *slope, dink, pinhead, chink*, and *WOG* when speaking of the North Vietnamese enemy, because such usage would be offensive to all Asians, regardless of political orientation or national origin. These orders, for the most part, were observed, although there were those who still referred to nearby ARVN units as "the local VC." There were, of course, other circumlocutions. One battalion commander, Lt. Colonel Reginald T. Lombard, dutifully passed on Westmoreland's order with appropriate conviction and then added, tongue in cheek: "From now on, the South Vietnamese will be referred to as 'Noble Allies.'" It was not long until one could hear radio operators referring to South Vietnamese Army units as the NAs or "November Alphas."

If there was concern over what one said and how one said it at the cutting edge of the Army, there was even more concern about what the military said and to whom in Washington.

Speak Only When Spoken To and Then Only...

Mr. McNamara was not happy with the provisions of the National Security Act which gave the Joint Chiefs of Staff a channel to express their views to the president and to the Congress. Mr. McNamara was confident that whatever the president or the Congress needed to know that the secretary of defense could convey the message. Title 10 U.S. Code, Section 137(e) provides: "After first informing the Secretary of Defense, a member of the Joint Chiefs of Staff may make such recommendations to Congress relating to the Department of Defense as he may consider appropriate." On January 11, 1965, McNamara had Deputy Secretary Cyrus Vance produce a memorandum to the Joint Chiefs of Staff detailing how they must conduct themselves before Congress. First—and only if asked by one of the members of the committee holding the hearing—the Joint Chiefs of Staff member must state whether or not he had already raised the issue under discussion with appropriate authorities in the Department of Defense. Next, he must state that, despite his personal differences with official DOD policy, that he is willing to abide by "the departmental position," and thirdly—then and only then—the Joint Chiefs of Staff member may expound his own view, provided he also gives an accurate portrayal of the arguments supporting the DOD policy.

These rules placed the initiative to discover differences of opinion between the members of the Joint Chiefs of Staff and the Department of Defense in the hands of Congress. Admiral Anderson and General LeMay, by their congressional appearances, may have provoked the DOD policy memo of January 11, 1965. Both men were quite frank in telling the Congress when they did not agree with Mr. McNamara. Even if their actions did not cause McNamara to publish a formal memo on how they should address the Congress, the circumstances of their departure certainly enhanced the chances of its observance. Admiral Anderson was retired at the end of his first two-year term. LeMay was extended for only what was to be a one-year extension after this first term, but to keep LeMay from being free to assist Senator Barry Goldwater in his 1964 presidential campaign, LeMay was extended another eight months. Thus, although in disfavor, he did not retire until January 1965.

There is, indeed, a certain logic in having the Defense Department speak with one voice, but there are dangers as well. McNamara established himself as the final judge of contending military recommendations. He did not wish the views he had already rejected to be heard. That is an awesome responsibility for one man to shoulder and especially so when one considers the consequences of error to the individual serviceman on the battlefield and, perhaps, to the nation as a whole.

Given the possibility that one who has spent his life as a military professional might make an error in his own field, it would seem more prudent to have encouraged military policy debate rather than stifle it. Doing so along above-board channels might have been a great deal more useful than stimulating leaks to lawmakers at the Army Navy Club or on the golf course.

There was, perhaps, a bit of Admiral William Sims in Anderson and a bit of Billy Mitchell in LeMay, but as America embarked on its fourth major war of the century, the Sims, Mitchells, Andersons, and LeMays were either dead or retired. We would go to war marching in step with a civilian secretary of defense who was slow to resolve the debate over grand strategy and yet quick to grasp the levels of control over operational details.

Yielding the Torch

When the United States ground forces buildup in South Vietnam began in 1965, the Joint Chiefs of Staff had a clear idea of what they planned to do in Vietnam and the troops that would be needed to carry out their plans. They began on March 20, 1965, soon after the return of Army Chief of Staff Harold K. Johnson from his fact-finding trip for President Johnson, with a recommendation for a major troop deployment. From the outset, it was clear that the Joint Chiefs of Staff wanted to win in Vietnam and were not interested in a holding action: "The level of force which they recommended to carry out this aggressive mission and which they saw as an essential component of the broader program to put pressure on the DRV/VC and to deter Chinese Communist aggression, was three divisions, one ROK and two U.S." Expressing themselves in JCSM 321–65, dated April 30, 1965, it was apparent that the Joint Chiefs of Staff were advocating the aggressive use of three full divisions; however, what the Chiefs were saying "was not in keeping with the cautious language of the 'Victory Strategy' sanctioned at the Honolulu Conference of 20 April." Basically, it had been decided in Honolulu to follow what had been described earlier in this book as a desist strategy. Thus, until June 7, 1965, the Joint Chiefs of Staff were ahead of the Department of Defense and General Westmoreland in pushing for an aggressive strategy and for three divisions or 27 battalions.

On June 7, 1965, however, General Westmoreland broke through the 27-battalion level with a request for the rapid deployment of 44 battalions. Westmoreland's action touched off a debate in which the Joint Chiefs of Staff were "caught in the middle between [Westmoreland] and the powerful and strident opposition his latest request for forces had surfaced in Washington."

From that date on, the Joint Chiefs of Staff were to lose ground in their role as participants in the war policy-making process. They probably did not mean to do so, but the battlefield along the Potomac became baffling, overpowering, and distracting.

First, they were baffled by the leadership style of a commander-in-chief whose war aims remained an enigma until March 31, 1968. They were overpowered by Mr. McNamara, his whiz kids, and the restraints placed upon their role as policy advocates and by McNamara's ability to determine budgets and strength levels. They were distracted by their duties as service chiefs who had to squeeze out somehow the forces needed by field commanders to meet not only the needs of an Asian ground war but also to meet the Sino-Soviet threat worldwide. As 1965 progressed, they increasingly lost control of the war in Vietnam to the White House/DOD combination in Washington and to the CINCPAC/ COMUSMACV combination in the Pacific and Southeast Asia.

It should be kept in mind that General Westmoreland was the man on the scene. It is only natural that he would be able to focus upon the requirements he needed to get his portion of the war accomplished in the shortest possible time. Likewise, the staff officers in Saigon had little to distract them from determining requirements for more forces and from putting in place the logistic machinery needed to make these forces combat effective. For them, there was no concern for what the armed forces were doing elsewhere. The shooting war was in Southeast Asia and by training they were disposed to bring it to a quick and successful conclusion. For them, there was no family to go home to at five o'clock. Indeed, General Westmoreland worked them 12-hour days at least, and Saturday and Sunday were just like the other days of the week. Under Westmoreland, the entire military effort in South Vietnam took on a driving dynamism that reflected Westmoreland's enthusiasm for doing any job as well as it could be done.

As time went on, the direction of the war became a dialectic between the theses proposed by Westmoreland's headquarters and the antitheses proposed by the commander-in-chief and the OSD. Westmoreland would generate his troop requirements and McNamara would fly to Saigon to whittle down Westmoreland's requirements to manageable levels. Once the new troop increments were agreed upon (always below the level that Westmoreland felt he needed to win), the president would bless them and then be able to say that he had never denied a request of his commander in the field. Technically, this was true until March 1968.

A major blow to early deployment of the balanced forces required in Vietnam was the Johnson Administration's decision in the summer of 1965 not to call up the reserve components of the Army—the U.S. Army Reserve and the National Guard—which until then had been counted upon in all planning for mobilization/expansion of the forces. One consequence was to decree that, by this default, the war would be fought almost exclusively by the then existing Active Army, augmented by conscripted recruits and brand-new lieutenants rushed through rapidly expanded officer candidate schools. This denial of trained elements in support was a blow to the morale of many reservists; it resulted in serious dilution of the Army's professional standards, including ultimately its responsiveness and discipline (Lt. Calley is a good example); and it may also have played a part in the subsequent alienation of the American public from what came to be called, as a term of opprobrium *the military*.

Denied mobilization, the Joint Chiefs of Staff had to scramble to produce even the incremental additions to United States forces in Southeast Asia. With the impetus for more troops coming from Saigon and the drive to hold down the manpower levels below the mobilization "sound barrier," the Joint Chiefs of Staff were whipsawed by their desire to see that Westmoreland got what he needed to win and by the enormous problems they had of taking his needs out of the hide of the other active components (including those in Europe). In the turmoil, they became like tiny tailors so busy making alterations to pieces of a suit that they had no time to influence its shape or style or to even look up. They could only hope that when they were told to quit sewing whatever they were making would fit.

"Ah, Les Statistiques!"

"Ah, les statistiques!" one of the Vietnamese generals exclaimed to an American friend. "Your Secretary of Defense loves statistics. We Vietnamese can give him all he wants. If you want them to go up, they will go up. If you want them to go down, they will go down," reported Roger Hilsman in *To Move a Nation*. In warfare, it is said that "truth is the first casualty." Nowhere was this truer than in the Vietnam War. Truth was under attack from the highest levels of government to the lowest element required to provide input into a report.

Hard facts about Vietnam were scarce enough. But, as the American involvement grew, what was known in Washington and Saigon became increasingly bent by the individual and bureaucratic drives of the humans caught up in the American effort.

At the top, studies were made and reports were written that reflected what key policy-makers wanted to hear. The scientific method of inquiry was prostituted to produce studies supporting an increasing American effort. For example, in 1964, when then Captain, USN, William P. Mack was serving on the Joint Staff, he was detailed to prepare papers for use by General Maxwell D. Taylor:

> General Taylor, as CJCS, was head of the Special Group-Counterinsurgency and I was in the joint staff—the guy who prepared all the papers for General Taylor. General [Victor] Krulak, a Marine General, was the special assistant for counterinsurgency. He was really the main cog between McNamara, Bobby Kennedy and those in Vietnam. He would go on out, make an assessment for McNamara, come back and I would have to prepare the Joint Staff papers which would reflect what he found out there and this would be the next six month's budget and plan for what was to happen.... I went through about three of those and the last one was the famous 1964 paper where Mr. McNamara came back [from Vietnam] and said: "Now we're going to prepare a plan. It's going to be the plan to end all plans. Whatever we want we're going to do. We are going to train so many people in language capability and all the rest of these things and that's going to be the job that's going to end the war in December." At that time I asked General Krulak, "Well what do you think? I must put some assumptions in this paper. You were out there.

What assumptions should we use?" He said, "Don't worry about the assumptions, put down the end result." Well, that's a hell of a way to work a paper—backwards. He said, "This is what the President wants. This is what Bobby Kennedy wants. This is what the Special Group–Counterinsurgency wants. This is what General Taylor is going to give them and you have to prepare a paper which has the conclusion they want so it has to be worked backwards to the assumptions." "Well, I can't put assumptions in because they won't track. If I put the assumptions in, true assumptions, you'll get a different conclusion. I can't lie.

If you want to put assumptions in—you were the one who was out there—you put them in." So, in the end, he put them in, and I worked the paper and it went over and that's the famous Taylor report that came out. I was protesting all the way that this was wrong.... Now McNaughton was being fed all this study in ISA ... foreordained conclusions without anything to back them up.

If intellectual dishonesty was being practiced at the top, the situation was not enhanced by the quality of the reports coming from the field. The decision-makers in Washington only had two sources of information and both had some inherent, but understandable, flaws. They were the functionaries of the United States government, e.g., the CIA, the DIA, the State Department, and, of course, the press. The press will be discussed later.

The first flaw in the governmental reporting was the nature of the systems demanded by Mr. McNamara and his civilian associates. By placing emphasis upon quantifiable inputs, the reporting systems tended to emphasize the quantifiable at the expense of the unquantifiable. This bias led to the exclusion or overlooking of significant elements of the Vietnamese puzzle. Secondly, as Brigadier General George D. Eggers, USA (Ret.) observed that

the move toward centralization was engendered by the personalities of the national level leaders and by the telecommunications capability which enabled senior civilian and military officials to monitor and direct activities on a worldwide, round the clock basis. Tactical commanders lost much of the flexibility they had enjoyed previously and became acutely aware of their increased exposure to superiors whose perceptions and judgments would influence their professional advancement.

Added to this increased exposure was the Army's self-inflicted problem of short command tours for company, battalion, and brigade commanders. The rationale which limited these commanders to a six-month stint in command was to give command experience to a large number of officers. On its face, this policy had the apparent merit of building a large cadre of combat experienced commanders, but its true overriding purpose was to meet the criteria of promotion boards that were instructed to look for officers with "successful" command on their records.

V. Riverine Warfare—On the Potomac

The result of this rather calculating approach to the direction of young Americans in battle is reflected by General Eggers: "The short duration of these tours exacerbated the problem of over centralization. Commanders had to master the rudiments of their job and produce career enhancing results in a tragically brief period of time.... Commanders felt that they had to 'look good' quickly and consistently."

In a war with no front lines and in which a great deal of the reporting was done by word-of-mouth over the radio, the temptation and the opportunity to stretch the truth was great. Unsurprisingly, a blood trail left by a retreating enemy soldier often became evidence that he would eventually die unobserved out in the jungle. An actual NVA or VC body miraculously multiplied by a factor of two or more in the burial process. Sometimes, unburied enemy were happened upon by a succession of patrols, each eager to claim credit for what was probably the work of artillery, an airstrike, disease, or even old age. Enemy weapons were reported as captured and then somehow lost in the evacuation process to higher headquarters. Often, it was surmised they were stolen by souvenir hunters or the helicopter crews transporting them. It was not uncommon for some units to lug around an extra AK-47 rifle or two to report captured when a contact produced no or little results. When there were Americans killed in action, there was a great temptation to overestimate losses to the other side. Sometimes, this was rationalized as necessary for the morale of the troops not close enough to the action to know what really happened, other than that some of their buddies were killed.

Even the way the enemy were killed could be distorted by ambition. One general officer who was reassigned from the flat and almost treeless Mekong Delta region to the dense jungles northwest of Saigon could not understand why his new unit was not killing any NVA with sniper rifles. The reason was obvious to any soldier who had been in the jungles, where seeing front sight of one's own rifle could be a challenge. The general continued to complain about the paucity of sniper kills until one battalion commander began to report a great deal of success in this area. No one ever questioned the rather large holes in these bodies (which could not have been made by mere rifle fire) and when this commander's six months in command were over, he was moved to a prized staff assignment. Later, in 1979, he was promoted to higher command.

Failure to play the numbers game could have a disastrous impact on the careers of those who refused to do so. Some battalion and company commanders would not report enemy dead unless they could "step on them." If they were fortunate and were at the place and time when the enemy wanted to fight, they had no trouble providing the numbers to support the reporting system's appetite for enemy KIA and enemy weapons figures. Those who hit a dry spell and whose immediate superior was thirsting to look good found themselves out of a job even before the short six-month tour was over.

The implications upon the officer corps of rewarding dishonesty and punishing honesty will be discussed in more detail in Chapter VII, but one must fear that the Army's "mirror-image" selection process will perpetuate this evil for some time to come.

To intellectual dishonesty and personal ambition must be added the other human factors of error, fatigue, and a certain amount of *ennui* as the war wore on with no apparent military objective in sight. Air Force General Milton recalled one of McNamara's reports:

> He had this report ... which came through the computers every day from Vietnam to Washington. This was: body count, captured rifle count, captured mess kits, God, I don't know what all. It was utterly meaningless data to be going into Washington—the name of the squadron commander of every squadron, the name of the commander of the destroyer on Yankee Station running the carrier screen. All this stuff went in every day to Washington and it gave them the feeling that they knew more about the war than the guys who were out there. They had all this detail. And they really knew, they ... knew that there were 1114 rifles captured yesterday. What they didn't know was that some tired sergeant late one evening just put down any goddamn figure he felt like putting down because he had to have a report.

There is a saying among computer programmers: "Garbage in, garbage out." Mr. McNamara and his computer-oriented assistants should have made more allowance for the human factors that can cause a computer to be loaded with hastily compiled and often wrong data. As General William E. DePuy, one of the Army's foremost thinkers, explained. "Soldiers in the Pentagon or on the battlefield generally try their damndest to respond to orders. If the civilian leaders ask for a report in two days, they get it—exactly two days' worth."

At the risk of understatement, it can be said that United States military operations in Vietnam were not conducted under favorable conditions either to defeat the enemy or to cause him to desist. The commander charged with the responsibility for the war in South Vietnam (General Westmoreland) was not stationed at the place (Washington, D.C.) where the really important decisions were being made. He was not given command of all the forces operating within his area of responsibility, not to mention adjacent countries. From the outset of the United States ground troop involvement, there was no clear statement of United States war aims. Thus, the military strategy evolved for use in South Vietnam was a compromise that gave the appearance of fitting within the framework of the grand strategies of "defeat" and "desist." Day-to-day operational decisions bearing upon the progress of the war inside Vietnam were made half a world away by men with no real military experience or expertise. Political pressures and constraints overwhelmed and reduced the Joint Chiefs of Staff to being only individual service chiefs, stripping their services worldwide to find the means to fight a prolonged war in Southeast Asia. No one really knew the war's progress or lack thereof because the reporting system was faulty, tended to focus upon the quantifiable at the expense of other important factors and eventually lost its integrity.

But the conditions under which the war was conducted are only a portion of the equation. In the next chapter, the means available to achieve the aims of policy and several factors influencing the availability of adequate means to achieve the aims of policy will be examined.

VI

Troops, Time, Tet,
and Truth

...that the work of strategy be allotted adequate means.
—Sound Military Decision

The war along the Potomac determined the conditions under which the military had to work in the Pentagon and in Southeast Asia. But, in addition, there began a debate within the nation about the wisdom of the Vietnam War policy and about the way in which it was being conducted. President Johnson, the politician, knew that the people wrote his fitness report as commander-in-chief. If he could accomplish the aims of policy at an acceptable cost and before the public's patience was exhausted, he would get a high mark.

In reality, President Johnson was dealing with three variables: the public's understanding of his war policy, the means they were willing to expend, and the amount of time the public would allot to the effort. To succeed, Johnson would have to be exceedingly able at reaching the public: in person, through the propaganda organs of the U.S. government, and through the media.

Public understanding and acceptance of his policy would determine, in large measure, the other two variables of troops and time. Johnson's task was difficult at best and was made more difficult because he did not possess either the military or diplomatic initiative. As a consequence, Hanoi, resting securely in the shadow of the Sino-Soviet threat to the United States, could manipulate the variable of time and, when it wished, could provoke crises on the American side by raising sharply the level of conflict and thus the cost in American lives. The enemy attacks at Tet 1968 provoked a decisive crisis in the Johnson Administration—a crisis breaking in the dimension of time that would further limit the means that would be allotted to the work of strategy.

To Mobilize or Not to Mobilize

Although President Johnson refused to mobilize our military's reserve components on Monday, July 26, 1965, the JCS continued to hope President Johnson would change his mind and thus:

> the great debate within the administration in 1967 was over the conduct of the ground war and that debate resolved around one crucial factor—mobilization. When the President began to search for the elusive point at which the costs of Vietnam would become unacceptable to the American people he always settled upon mobilization, the point at which reserves would have to be called up to support a war that was becoming increasingly distasteful to the American public. This constraint, with all its political and social repercussions, not any argument about strategic concepts of the "philosophy" of the war, dictated American war policy—Herbert Y. Schandler, in *The Unmaking of a President*.

From the beginning of United States military history, there has been a debate as to how the nation should raise its defense forces. One side, impelled by Federalist philosophy and best articulated by Emory Upton, argued for an exclusively federal force under the command of the President of the United States as commander-in-chief. The other side, in the van of Jeffersonian thought, and best articulated by John McAuley Palmer, pushed for a reserve force composed of the militias of the several states and only a small full-time force under the president.

This debate was never resolved to everyone's satisfaction and resulted, as is so often the case, in a compromise. For most of our history we have needed only a small establishment of "regulars" and a large force of reserves. The reserves themselves have been a mixture of the militias of each state organized as the National Guard and under the peacetime command of each state governor plus the federally controlled Army, Air Force, Naval, and Marine Reserves.

The National Guard holds the preponderance of Army combat power, i.e., divisions, regiments, brigades, and battalions of infantry, armor, and artillery. The Reserve forces have provided mostly Army service support units, i.e., quartermaster, finance, and postal detachments.

During the Cold War, the regular forces grew much larger than had been the norm but the National Guard and the reserves still played a key role in backing up the regulars as demonstrated in the Korean War and in the Berlin Crisis of 1961.

But the complaints of some reserve component personnel activated in the Berlin Crisis caused Mr. McNamara to question the validity of the reserve component concept. Subsequently, he made several partially successful attempts to reduce the size of the reserve components and to consolidate their units into what he saw as smaller, less expensive, and more effective organizational structures. Thus, despite the howls of governors and congressmen, many reserve component units were reduced from divisions to brigades and some units were eliminated altogether.

Nevertheless, at the start of the Vietnam War, the reserve components were still a formidable force-in-being, although the readiness of individual units ranged from outstanding to poor. The Air National Guard, for example, has always been the most combat ready of the reserve components. This has been due to the high caliber of the men and women who are attracted to and have the skills needed to function in this highly technical environment. It is also because the basic proficiency of air units is relatively easy to gauge. The hazards of aerial flight are such in both peace and war that low proficiency is quickly manifested in a high loss rate.

The Army National Guard's and Army Reserves' proficiency has been more difficult to assess simply because much of what infantry and armor units are supposed to be able to do in combat is difficult to test except in actual combat. Attempts to make their peacetime training realistic have always run headlong into an equally convincing case for safety. Artillery units, on the other hand, are much easier to judge because for them the test is to place a certain number of shells, upon a designated spot within a specified time. This testing can be accomplished readily and safely in designated training areas.

Thus, for defense planners, the actual value of the reserve components has always been somewhat of a puzzle. McNamara did not like puzzles, and since the military could not assign nice clean numbers for factoring the value of the reserve components, their importance to McNamara was dubious, indeed.

President Johnson had his own reasons to be cautious about how he dealt with the reserve components. First of all, without a declaration of war, he could only, by law, place the reserves on active duty for a period of up to one year. In addition, a reserve mobilization would automatically, by law, extend the length of service for those men already conscripted by one year. Thus, if President Johnson were to call up the reserves without a declaration of war or some special act from the Congress, the timing of the call-up would have to be precise if the enemy were to be defeated within the time frame the reserves would be available to serve.

President Johnson's other alternative was to ask for a declaration of war. However, that would slow down his Great Society programs, as the entire nation would have to go on a war footing until the state of emergency was over. Butter might have to give way to guns.

To ask Congress for a declaration of war would bring on an open debate over United States war aims and strategy. The people might express themselves through the Congress as not seeing our stake in Vietnam as vital. If so, the public would be repudiating an involvement begun by Democrat Harry S. Truman, who sent a military advisory group to Vietnam at the outset of the Korean War, and which had been deepened most dramatically and recently by two successive Democratic administrations. President Eisenhower refused to get American troops involved with France's Indo-China War.

Failure to get a declaration of war would mean "no confidence" in the HST-JFK-LBJ foreign policy in Southeast Asia and the probability of a Republican landslide in the next national election.

Indeed, there were many important reasons that kept the commander-in-chief and his secretary of defense from favoring a general reserve component mobilization, either with or without a declaration of war. Thus, the Johnson Administration would rest its actions on the Gulf of Tonkin Resolution that it rushed through Congress in 1964. Once armed with this almost unanimous expression of Congressional approval for a firm stand against communist aggression in Southeast Asia, President Johnson was unwilling to run the risk of a formal Congressional repudiation of his Vietnam policies.

To Lyndon Johnson, the consummate politician, there was only one choice: to send the American military to fight a "war during peace." Johnson failed to understand (or was not told in ways that he could understand) that the war plans and organization of his armed forces, since World War II, rested upon the assumption that a major land war anywhere in the world would automatically bring on a general mobilization of America's reserve components.

The Reserve Dilemma

It was increasingly clear during the spring and early summer of 1965 that a major force would be deployed in Vietnam. All the JCS plans assumed the use of reserve forces in the event of a major deployment. When the July 26, 1965, decision to deploy was announced, together with the decision not to declare a mobilization of some reserve component forces, the Army was confronted with a problem of unknown dimensions. The problem was especially acute because the entire Army force structure was based upon a predominantly combat arms active component with combat support and combat service support units provided by the reserve components. Without a mobilization, the Army would have to establish, organize, equip and train support units that did not even exist in the active Army structure. The leadership and skills in a force of approximately one million were spread eventually across a force that grew to more than one and a half million. Thus, if the Vietnam operations were to be supported, the needed support units would have to come out of the hide of the Active Army.

Army Chief of Staff General Harold K. Johnson, by dint of his superb administrative skills, was able to fashion a new support Army by stretching the Army's hide to fit. However, to the dismay of the JCS, they were not able to get President Johnson and Secretary McNamara to order the mobilization they felt was so badly needed if the United States was to win in Vietnam. What success they had in this regard was limited; over the long course of the war, only a little more than 23,000 members of the reserve components were called up on a selective basis. Some, but not all, of these individuals and units were actually deployed to Southeast Asia. Although they performed well overall, the reserve component call-up was token at best, and did not prevent the Army from having to conduct an almost complete internal overhaul at great cost in money and morale. In short, the active Army had to do the things the taxpayer had been paying for the reserve components to do in time of war.

As a consequence of the policies of the Johnson Administration, the members of the active components found themselves returning repeatedly to fight in Vietnam. Each time they went back to Vietnam, they met a new group of conscripts who were beginning to wonder why they were doing all the fighting while their contemporaries were riding college deferments or were being draft deferred by joining the reserve components or by becoming FAA air traffic controllers. Paradoxically, both became a means of escaping the draft.

Indeed, the conscripts who fought in Vietnam were not, in the academic-degree sense, the best educated that America had to offer—they were simply unqualified to be exempt from the draft. Remaining behind walls of ivy and armory walls was an upper class too rich and/or too smart to be conscripted. In time, some of the exempted experienced a certain amount of guilt and began to articulate a variety of reasons to end the war.

VI. Troops, Time, Tet, and Truth

As time passed, the active components lost, through reorganization, many fine officers and non-commissioned officers who could see no future in leading the unwilling to do what seemed pointless and unnecessary and, as the pointlessness of the war became manifest, the conscripts reflected the general unrest in the population. Lack of discipline, drugs, and "fragging" of unpopular officers and NCOs were the inevitable results—consequences that spread throughout the Army worldwide. By 1969, there was cause to wonder whether the Army could be counted upon as an instrument of either foreign policy or domestic security.

Some of the best-trained and highly motivated Army units in existence were to be found in the not-to-be-mobilized Selected Reserve Force (SRF). Among the old-timers in the National Guard, the sentiment was hawkish and from the powerful National Guard Association on down to the senior officers and NCOs of the National Guard, the attitude was to train hard and be ready to go finish the job for the active components, just as they had done in World War II and in the Korean War.

Paradoxically, many of the younger draft-motivated members of the Guard were members only in order to avoid going to war. In time, this led to friction within the reserve components. When public support for the Vietnam War collapsed, many of the hardline Guardsmen either gave up or quit. As a result, the once high standards of the SRF began to fall. That plummet in proficiency was accompanied by a rise in a feeling of shame on the part of some for not being mobilized and by the humiliation of being called, by some, a haven for draft dodgers.

That the reserve components were having serious recruiting and retention problems today should come as no surprise. The mismanagement of the nation's reserve component assets during the Vietnam War could have had no other result. There was still a hard core of dedicated old-timers in the reserve components, but it was almost impossible to attract the kind of idealistic, dedicated, young person needed to fill their ranks. The bitterness of Vietnam turned many against the military, in general. The "hiding place for draft dodgers" reputation still exists, even though there is no longer a draft to dodge or a draft to motivate enlistments.

There was also less incentive to join either the active or reserve components because, as is the case after every war, the benefits given by an initially grateful people are always cut back once the danger has passed. The military find themselves badgered on one side to recruit and retain an all-volunteer force and embattled on the other side as they try to preserve the pay, allowance, and retirement system that has been one of their most effective recruiting and retention lures. These cuts have always come at the end of wars the United States has won and thus no one should be particularly surprised if they are especially deep at the end of a war lost.

The No-Win Decision

At first, the United States ground forces in South Vietnam played a relatively passive role, but as they became accustomed to the climate and the terrain, General Westmoreland was more willing for them to carry the fight to the enemy. At first, the enemy appeared willing to try the American forces on for size. The first major battle took place in the Central Highlands along the Ia Drang River in October–November 1965 (when the 1st Air Cavalry Division decimated the 32nd, 33nd and 66th NVA Regiments, killing more than 1,771 of the enemy). Those regiments withdrew west of Du Co into Cambodia to lick their wounds until October 1966 when they took on the 1st Air Cavalry Division once again. That time, in a 25-day operation, the NVA lost 809 KIA and once again withdrew into Cambodia. It should be noted that the next operation in that same area lasted 74 days, resulting in NVA KIA of 977.

Applying a little analysis to the figures shows that in the fall of 1965, the 1st Air Cavalry Division was killing the NVA at the rate of 70.8 per day. The next year against the same regiments in the same battle area, the rate had fallen to 32.3 per day, and for the rest of 1966 in that same area two and one-third divisions (1st Air Cavalry, 4th Infantry Division and a brigade of the 25th Infantry Division) could only kill 13.2 NVA per day. Thus, the NVA were tying up the elements of three U.S. divisions in Pleiku Province and still staying well within acceptable loss rates. In the mountain forests and jungles of Pleiku Province, the NVA was difficult to find and, when the pressure became too heavy, it was easy for the NVA to slip across the border to the sanctuary of Cambodia. The folly of sanctuary warfare became more manifest but was still unheeded, as it is today in the Middle East and Afghanistan.

Clearly if the war in Vietnam were to be won, a large increase in the number of United States troops would be needed; however, at first, General Westmoreland obtained more combat troops than he could accommodate. The limiting factors were the lack of adequate port facilities, airfields, and logistical installations to handle the flow of combat forces and to sustain them with needed ammunition, petroleum products, and food. As long as there was this physical limitation to the number of troops that Westmoreland could accept, the Johnson Administration did not have to come to grips with the question of just how many troops it was willing to produce and dispatch to Vietnam. This limitation also helped the administration to avoid the question as to its war aims in Vietnam. Thus, the issue of whether the United States was trying to defeat the enemy as the military wanted to do or whether the United States was merely trying to make the enemy desist did not have to be resolved right away.

However, by the fall of 1966, the energetic efforts of Brigadier General John "Jumping Jack" Norton, who commanded the United States Army Support Command, Vietnam, were paying off. Norton drove his troops and civilian construction workers mercilessly to complete the logistical support facilities needed to permit the introduction of the forces needed to carry the war to the enemy throughout Vietnam. Thus, by August 5, 1966, the military could ask for troops that would permit them to seize the initiative. These projections called for an in-country troop strength of 542,588 or 90 maneuver battalions by the end of calendar year 1967.

Now, the issue was joined. Westmoreland's ability to accept and deploy troops was bumping against the administration's ability or willingness to provide the needed troops. Therefore, McNamara subjected the August 1966 request to a line-by-line review. On November 11, 1966, he announced that only 470,000 troops would be sent to Vietnam by June 1968, rather than the 542,588 asked for by the end of 1967.

What had happened to the President Johnson who stated publicly and often that he would give his commander in the field what he needed to prevail? Clearly, the troop requests were approaching or had penetrated the "mobilization sound barrier." Thus, the issue became: Do we mobilize and provide the troops to defeat the enemy or do we not mobilize and formally embrace the desist strategy?

McNamara in his announcement of November 11, 1966, articulated the two conflicting strategies and opted for one of them:

> to continue in 1967 to increase friendly forces as rapidly as possible, and without limit, and employ them primarily in large scale "seek out and destroy" operations to destroy the main force VC/NVA units ... [or] to follow a similarly aggressive strategy of "seek out and destroy," but to build friendly forces only to that level required to neutralize the large enemy units and prevent them from interfering with the pacification program....
>
> I believe it is time to adopt the second approach for three reasons: (1) If MACV estimates of enemy strength are correct, we have not been able to attrit the enemy forces fast enough to break their morale and more U.S. forces are unlikely to do so

in the foreseeable future; (2) we cannot deploy more than 470,000 personnel by the end of 1967 without a high probability of generating a self-defeating runaway inflation in SVN; and (3) endless escalation of U.S. deployments is not likely to be acceptable in the U.S. or to induce the enemy to believe that the U.S. is prepared to stay as long as is required to produce a secure non-communist SVN ... if enemy strength is greatly overstated and our ... operations have been more effective than our strength and loss estimates imply ... more than 470,000 U.S. personnel should not be required to neutralize the VC/NVA main force.

It is interesting to note that McNamara dealt with the mobilization issue only tangentially when he touched upon what would be "acceptable in the U.S." Yet, the mobilization issue was really the crux of the matter. Repeatedly, the Joint Chiefs of Staff tried to make it clear to Secretary McNamara that they could not meet Vietnam force requirements to win the war in a time and cost-effective manner without a mobilization, nor could they meet their other worldwide force requirements. Of special concern were the commitments to NATO.

Rather than deal with the political issue of mobilization, McNamara's staff attacked the troop strength issue in isolation from the issue of isolating the battlefield. Obviously, the number of troops needed to defeat the enemy in South Vietnam was related to the enemy's ability to reinforce with fresh troops and to the enemy's ability to arm and supply those troops. For the military strategy of attrition to work, the battlefield would have to be isolated. Without this isolation, the United States would be operating what Norman Hannah called a "meat grinder" operation. Thus, as Hannah suggests, the question would be "Who would tire first, he who feeds the machine or he who grinds?"

One of the simplest military axioms is to "attack your opponent's weakness, not his strength." Hanoi's greatest strength was its ability to feed meat into the machine. Mr. McNamara was telling the Joint Chiefs of Staff in November 1966, that the military would have to be content to operate the meat grinder in South Vietnam with 470,000 troops.

Secretary McNamara went on at great length in his memorandum of November 1966, to prove with charts and graphs that increasing the troop level beyond the 470,000 level would just result in an increased infiltration by the NVA. In two short (but revealing) paragraphs, he deals with infiltration and air interdiction. Noting that the rate of infiltration was rising and that the ratio of NVA to VC on the battlefield was also rising, he pointed out that the NVA units, equipped almost exclusively with Chinese and Russian weapons, have a much greater requirement for infiltrated ammunition and supplies, thus increasing their dependence on the logistics network flowing from NVN to SVN.

However, he concludes by saying, "But at the scale we are now operating, I believe our bombing is yielding very small marginal returns, not worth the cost in pilot lives and aircraft."

Significantly omitted from this memo is any discussion of what other means might be employed to prevent the supplies needed by the NVA from entering North Vietnam in the first place. Nor is there any discussion of the relationship between United States aircraft losses and the antiaircraft guns and MiG fighters that the North Vietnamese had to import from Sino-Soviet sources in order to cause these losses.

Now the strategy debate was out in the open, but it was decidedly one-sided. Each member of the Joint Chiefs of Staff was a service chief with tremendous responsibilities worldwide, and, without the mobilization their plans called for, they would have to work even harder to produce what was needed in Southeast Asia while keeping a wary eye upon Europe and other concerns. To those burdens were now added the burden of being on the defensive in dealing with OSD on the issue of troop strength. The systems analysts began to pick at each troop request and to deal with it as if the other factors involved in grand and military strategy did not exist. There was no way the Joint Chiefs of Staff could ever win because they were trying to amass what was needed to defeat the enemy, while McNamara and OSD were committed to holding the line short of mobilization. The only way the enemy might have been defeated without a large mobilization would have been for the enemy to make a serious mistake.

Inexplicably, General Vo Nguyen Giap did just that. In January 1968, he threw the full weight of the VC, backed by the NVA, into an all-out attack in South Vietnam. In so doing, he presented the United States with the opportunity to defeat the NVA/VC that supposedly had been lost with the November 1966 decision to level off at 470,000 troops and try to wait the enemy out.

Tet, 1968—An Opportunity Lost

In warfare, as in football, the winner is usually the side that makes fewer mistakes. There is another truism: he who maintains the initiative can often force his opponents into making errors. Both Washington and Hanoi made their share of mistakes, but with the strategic initiative largely in the hands of the North Vietnamese, the United States, although it could bring a certain amount of military pressure to bear inside South Vietnam, could never wrest the diplomatic or political initiative away from Hanoi.

Washington seemed to be forever waiting for Hanoi's reaction to a bombing start or a bombing stop or to a formula in a speech or to some message sent through some circuitous diplomatic channel. Because the North Vietnamese had clearly defined war aims, the means to carry them out and, thanks to United States' fears of Sino-Soviet reaction, could wage war in South Vietnam under favorable conditions, they did not have to react to United States actions or proposals. Only when they saw an advantage to be gained did the North Vietnamese deign to respond to United States signals.

The rationale behind the Tet 1968 offensive is, even in retrospect, difficult to understand. It would endow General Giap with prescience to posit that he could have predicted the media would report the NVA/VC defeat as a victory for North Vietnam. It is more likely that Giap believed, mistakenly, that the Tet '68 attacks would succeed and result in a defeat of the Free World Forces. All men are subject to dreams and generals are none the less so. Alternatively, he may have thought that Tet '68 provided the ARVN/U.S. with the opportunity to destroy the local VC, and save Giap the trouble after his eventual all-out invasion and conquest of South Vietnam. Either way, General Giap must have thought he had a lot to gain.

In what may be one of history's most remarkable paradoxes, Giap's forces were soundly defeated throughout South Vietnam. The GVN did not fold and the South Vietnamese armed forces, down to and including the Regional Force/Popular Forces elements, fought astonishingly well. Unfortunately, the initial successes of the attack, which took advantage of the principle of surprise during the most important Vietnamese holiday, created the illusion of a communist victory. The Battle of Tet 1968 was, in fact a terrible disaster for the NVA/VC. The VC were virtually wiped out and were, according to recent reports from Hanoi "no longer a factor in the war," from that time on. *Paradoxically, the media reported Tet 1968 as a great victory for the Communists and a great defeat for the Free World Forces.*

Apparently, Generals Wheeler and Westmoreland understood what had happened but could not make the decision-makers in Washington understand it as well. McNamara's reporting system should have been able to assess the damage to both sides, and thus the decision-makers could have discounted the inaccurate reports coming from the media. But the media were quicker, further eroding the crumbling public support for the war effort. If there were ever a time to mobilize the reserve components and pile on, it was when the VC infrastructure had been either killed or exposed. Tet 1968 was the moment of truth when a successful combatant with the killer instinct should and would have gone all out to defeat his opponent.

The Battle of the Bulge was a near thing for the Allies in World War II, but on the battlefield was a Patton with the entire Third United States Field Army, which General Omar Bradley could divert to repair the rip in the Allied lines and exploit the situation. In Vietnam, at Tet, the enemy was soundly thrashed by the troops on hand, but there was no Third Field Army to come and pile on. It would have had to be dispatched from the United States in concert with a general mobilization.

But the exploitation forces were never sent because the United States public had lost the will to continue and because it understood Tet 1968 as an enemy victory rather than an enemy defeat.

Chicken Little Meets the Albatross

> *Historians ... have concluded that the Tet offensive resulted in a severe military-political setback for Hanoi in the South. To have portrayed such a setback for one side as a defeat for the other—in a major crisis abroad—cannot be counted as a triumph for American journalism.*
> —Peter Braestrup in *Big Story: How the American Press and Television Reported and Interpreted the Crisis of Tet in 1968 in Vietnam and Washington*

Although there was some exceptionally good reportage of the war in Vietnam, the overall effort of the media was handicapped by the inexperience of the reporters who covered the war. Due to their inexperience, they often failed to grasp the importance or the lack of importance of what they saw or heard. There were enormous pressures upon these young men and women to file stories or to whip together commentary for news film that would make deadlines and would have sufficient visual impact to merit some exposure on the evening TV news shows. For these reasons, there was a tendency on the part of the media to run out and take films of whatever might appear spectacular and yet remain near the communications and transportations links to the United States. As a result, the sensational and conveniently nearby stories were often filed at the expense of stories of greater significance. In his article, "It Takes More Than Talent to Cover a War," in the July 1978 issue of *Army*, Col. William V. Kennedy wrote,

> When the late S.L.A. Marshall arrived on the scene, he reported that "the over-whelming majority [of the reporters] did not get to the front ... there is a cynical faddishness to war reporting out of Vietnam that contrasts diametrically with prior performance.... Today's correspondent prefers a piece that will make people squirm and agonize. Never before ... has there been so much concentration on the off-beat yarn to the exclusion of balanced accounting of how ... operations are being conducted.

There were a few brave and patient reporters, most notably, Joseph L. "Joe" Galloway, who would actually take the time and risk to walk through the jungle with the American rifle companies. But for the most part, the young reporters would try to pick the brains of the intelligence and the operations officers at division level and above for stories about United States military operations. Such inanities as "How's the war going?" "How's the enemy's morale" or "How's the morale of our troops?" were all too typical. Operations officers had little problem describing the location and nature of on-going operations. Basically, all an operations officer could say, in all honesty, was that the maneuver units were doing their best to kill or capture the enemy in their assigned sectors of operation. Of course, future operations could rarely be discussed.

The only meaningful question to be asked of an operations officer was: "Is your area clear or not clear of the enemy today?" In truth, the answer would have to be either "no" or "I don't know." The second answer would be applicable to the days when there was no enemy contact and the first answer applicable to days when fighting was taking place. The point is that operations officers could not predict the future course of the war even in their own areas of operation. All they, and the troops out combing the jungle, could do was keep trying. As long as the NVA/VC held the initiative, there was no way to predict the end of the war. If the media were to discover the answer, it was fishing at the wrong place. The length of the war would be determined in either Hanoi or in the United States. The media had virtually no access to the former and almost complete freedom with the latter. Under the circumstances, one could only hope the media would report whatever they saw as accurately as possible.

The intelligence officers, on the other hand, were the keepers of such data as the number of enemy killed or captured. It should be noted that the press was always asking for those figures. The charge of dealing in body counts should not be laid exclusively at the feet of the military. The press was quite eager to have this information as a measure of progress or lack of progress in a war in which the occupation of territory had little to do with who was winning.

Unfortunately, none or few reporters asked the intelligence officers the really important question: "Based on the enemy's ability to resupply and reinforce its units in your area of operations, how long will it take your division to eliminate the enemy from your area of operations?" The answer would have to have been, "Forever."

This same criticism can be leveled at the Johnson Administration. It was not until the commitment of American ground troops that some in the administration began to listen to the intelligence community's warnings that North Vietnam could produce enough persons of military age forever and that the Sino-Soviets could supply them enough arms to tie up over a half-million United States troops indefinitely.

No doubt a nation of then 212 million could defeat a nation of then 19 million, but a ratio of 10:1 or 15:1 in combat troops over the enemy plus the destruction of North Vietnam's war-making ability would have been required. Since North Vietnam actually made little of the hardware she required to wage war in the south, some of North Vietnam would have to have been occupied in order to seal it off from outside support.

The plight of those who provided official information to the press, the pressure of deadlines plus the lack of professionalism on the part of a young, ambitious and inexperienced corps of news people is readily understood. But one would have thought that back home the more mature owners of the media and their more detached and experienced editors would have made a greater attempt to achieve a measure of fairness and balance in presenting the war news to the public. Some, but not all, members of the Fourth Estate attempted to use *selective* reporting as a tool to form or alter United States foreign policy toward Southeast Asia.

Dr. Ernest W. Lefever conducted an analysis of the *CBS Evening News* during the period 1972–73 and found "that it employed selective reporting techniques to promote a position opposed to United States military involvement in Vietnam; failed to offer a fair picture of viewpoints contra to that of CBS News; failed to provide facts essential to public understanding of fundamental national security issues; ignored vital facts; overplayed others; and tended to fixate upon the trivial at the expense of the significant."

Does the press have a duty to present only the facts or does it also have the duty to try to form or alter governmental policy? Democratic theory says an informed electorate will effect whatever political changes it feels are proper. To try to manipulate public opinion by biased, slanted, or selective reporting implies a lack of belief in the characteristics that make democracies work. Just because the administration's spokesmen may try to present the administration's point of view in a biased manner does not mean that similar measures on the part of a free press are either necessary or desirable. The truth carries its own sword. It will pierce sham or deceit. It needs no help other than its mere exhibition. Willful distortion of the facts or the suppression of those facts that do not fit the views of the reporter or the desk man or the publisher is not in the public interest. This does not preclude analyses and interpretation by trained and experienced newspersons, provided they avoid the temptation of selective reporting.

The Fourth Estate has a vital mission. To perform it well, the press must observe the distinction between analysis and propaganda and not become the handmaiden of one particular political party.

There is no evidence that selective, biased, and unfair reporting shortened the United States involvement by one day. Indeed, given the personalities of Presidents Johnson and Nixon, such activities may have lengthened our involvement. Hanoi was not deceived by whatever the press or the administration said, but Hanoi may have been led by the Fourth Estate's attempt to make foreign policy to feel that the administration's position was weaker than it actually was. Thus, the American media may have hardened Hanoi at the negotiating table and thereby prolonged the time it took for the United States to work itself into a position from which it could withdraw from Vietnam.

The enemy offensive at Tet 1968 was a terrible shock to the Saigon press corps. First of all, many of the best reporters were either in South Korea covering the USS *Pueblo* story or were away on leave. Even so, there were some experienced correspondents such as Peter Arnett on hand:

The reason the press became so alarmed over the Tet attacks in Saigon was quite simple. Most of the reporters had never awakened in a situation in which apparently all hell was breaking loose around them. Thus, when daylight came and General Westmoreland was strolling along the grounds surrounding the American Embassy to view the bodies of the enemy sappers killed during their abortive attempt to get inside the embassy, the reporters could not believe Westmoreland's aura of calm. They felt he was putting on a front to hide the seriousness of the true situation. Nothing could have been more removed from the truth. Although General Westmoreland realized that the embassy was an important psychological target, it was of no particular significance when viewed in perspective. The enemy failed to get inside the embassy itself. Some broken glass and a few dead VC were not big news to Westmoreland, although to the reporters being so close to the action it must have seemed like a supreme adventure, wrote Braestrup, who was there at time.

In an article in *The Reporter*, Mr. [Hanson] Baldwin [military correspondent for *The New York Times*] wrote, "Some of the correspondents in Saigon are not capable of adequately reporting military operations. And some of the TV reporters have generalized editorial judgments that they have neither the competence nor the knowledge to sustain."

General Bruce C. Clarke, USA (Ret.) happened to be in Vietnam at the time of Tet 1968 and observed that "the enemy took the battle down around the Caravelle Hotel and, so from the standpoint of the average reporter over there, it was the acorn that fell on the chicken's head and it said, 'The sky is falling!'"

One can understand how in their eagerness to convey the excitement of the attacks taking place in Saigon that the reporters might have been a bit melodramatic and, in their haste, less than accurate, but as time went on and the situation became more clear, the insistence of some of them that the Free World Forces had been defeated is difficult to understand. Was it due to a personal bias or to the bias of their publishers? Peter Braestrup, who was on the scene and was initially just as confused as the others, concluded that most of the reporters simply were in error and misinterpreted what they were seeing. Braestrup damns some of his colleagues and especially rewrite men and editors back in the United States for persisting with the theme of an enemy victory long after the local reporters had seen their errors and had sent in correcting dispatches. The story of a Free World defeat simply snowballed and was a "better" story (for a good portion of the media) than was a Free World victory.

The full impact of the media failure to report Tet 1968 accurately and fairly may never be known, but it had a decisive impact on both the public and the elites in the United States. General William E. DePuy, who was one of three briefers to inform the Wise Men (a group of presidential advisers President Johnson assembled to assist in a Vietnam policy review on March 25, 1968), recalled, "George Ball asked Phil Habib if the war could be won militarily. Phil said, 'no!' In my opinion, that is the only message the group carried out of the room. By the way, the Wise Men had their minds made up long before their visit or at least most did." Almost all the Wise Men were out of the government and no longer had access to classified reports. They, like less notable citizens, had to rely upon the media for an accounting of what was happening in Southeast Asia.

97

"Ironically, if there were ever a time, up to that point, that the war could have been won militarily, it was in the spring of 1968," wrote DePuy.

When the Wise Men advised the president to withdraw from Vietnam, he took that advice. On March 31, 1968, in an address to the nation, President Johnson settled the strategy question once and for all. There would be no American "win" in Vietnam. Johnson had come full circle. If there were to be a victory of some sort, it would have to be won by Asian, not American, boys. If there were to be a different strategy, it would have to be the strategy of a new president. He was going back to the Texas hill country and try to figure out how he had gone wrong.

The American military has its My Lai—an albatross it must wear, even though My Lai was a rare exception. But the American media will have to wear the albatross of Tet 1968. Hopefully, the failure of the media at Tet will also be an exceptional phenomenon. But if the performance of the America media during and in the wake of the 2016 presidential election is any indication, that must give one pause.

Drawdown in Europe

The war in Vietnam caused the deterioration of United States forces worldwide. Space does not permit a command-by-command examination of the problem; however, by looking at the United States European Command (EUCOM), which before and after the Vietnam War held top priority for personnel, money, and equipment, the impact of the drawdown upon other commands of lower priority can be inferred.

As stated earlier, the United States Army, Europe (the major component of EUCOM) was at peak efficiency in the late 1950s and early 1960s under General Bruce C. Clarke and General Paul L. Freeman, Jr. Freeman recalled:

I returned from commanding U.S. Army Europe to take over Continental Army Command in April 1965—just as the decision was made to commit major combat elements into Southeast Asia. It was my responsibility to dismantle our fine STRAF (Strategic Army Force) and reconfigure it for Vietnam; to firm up the training and school base; to train and ship units and replacements; to open up long-closed officer candidate schools as a source for officers. Since the Reserve Components were denied to us in the first years of the conflict, none of these things were done as the military wanted to do them. There was political obstruction throughout.

VI. Troops, Time, Tet, and Truth

As General Freeman was stripping the Army's Strategic Forces from the continental United States, General Lyman L. Lemnitzer, who commanded NATO and EUCOM at that time, reported, "The transfer of personnel and material from Europe to VN substantially reduced the military capability of the U.S. Forces, Europe. There was a considerable drawdown of experienced personnel, talent and material. In the later years, however, the military capability of our personnel was improved by the transfer of large numbers of combat veterans to Europe who had completed their VN service." The officer and higher-ranking NCO returnees to the European theater were of benefit to EUCOM, but many of the more junior enlisted personnel arriving in Europe from Vietnam were a definite detriment to combat readiness, a fact that the NATO-level General Lemnitzer did not detect. First of all, they were mostly "short-timers"—men who only had less than a year to go before their period of conscription expired and they could return to civilian life. Secondly, some of them had begun to use drugs in Southeast Asia—a practice they continued in Europe. Thirdly, racial tensions, which had been lessened somewhat in Vietnam by the realization that enemy bullets penetrate both white and black skins and by the generally outstanding performance of black soldiers in combat, began to resurface outside of the combat zone. Fourth, the lack of money for ammunition and petroleum for maneuvers and a general equipment shortage reduced the time that could be given to training and increased the amount of time the troops had to spend in the barracks some of which were in deplorable condition. The old Wehrmacht-built barracks taken over by the United States forces at the end of World War II were literally falling on their heads. The plumbing was so calcified that urine backed up in the latrines and the few showers that worked drained down the interior walls.

Due to inflation induced by the Vietnam War, the dollar sank to new lows and the G.I. abroad found that even the newly increased pay scales would not buy him very much. Along with that, the German girls had little interest in the G.I.s anymore. They were more interested in the increasingly affluent German boys. The G.I.s, who used to literally leap at the chance to go downtown to chase the German girls, preferred to remain on the *Kaserne* and experiment with drugs. America and Americans had lost their attraction. Marrying a G.I. to get to come to America was passé. The Vietnam War was not a cause for pride and the Army that had whipped the Wehrmacht was not doing very well against a supposedly inferior enemy. The young Americans, who in earlier years had been such good language learners, and especially quick to learn the "du" form of German, found themselves unwilling to learn or unwilling to give up the language barrier as an excuse for not having a girlfriend.

Major General Adrian St. John II, who commanded the 14th Armored Cavalry Regiment along the East-West Border from 1967 to 1969 and then served as an assistant division commander of the 4th Armored Division in Germany, said:

> There was a significant impact by the war in Southeast Asia on all facets of readiness in U.S Army, Europe; it was a direct impact until about 1972. After 1972, it was an indirect impact. We were in the hole from the earlier low priority; but we began working our way up in 1972, and had achieved some momentum of improvement by 1974.... A lack of experienced people was a major difficulty.... Most company commanders were lieutenants on their first assignment and knew they were marking time before orders to Vietnam; the average time in command of my troop commanders in 1967 and 1968 was four and a half months.... Most were willing and intelligent; they just did not have time to learn their jobs or their men, nor was there adequate time nor sufficient experience throughout the next higher levels to teach them.... The adverse situation was similar with the NCOs.... Many were good combat leaders and had gotten their stripes quickly in Vietnam but lacked the experience for peace-time leadership.... I thought we were just barely holding our own ... until about mid–1969, and then everything started downhill at breakneck speed. Many of the newly-assigned soldiers brought race and drug problems with them; but conditions were so tenuous in Europe that, even if they were minor individual problems before, they rapidly spread and quickly became major problems.

General Bruce C. Clarke returned to Europe on various special missions during the Vietnam War and was appalled at the condition of the barracks, the appearance of the troops, their low morale, and their poor state of readiness. As the once proud United States Army, Europe became unready, the reason for it rested upon one word: Vietnam.

The demands of the war in Vietnam for young leaders and young enlisted persons were enormous. General Michael S. Davison, who commanded the United States Army, Europe in the early 1970s, commented:

> The war in Southeast Asia had a severe impact on the combat readiness of U.S. Army, Europe. Probably the single greatest factor contributing to the deterioration of combat readiness was the extreme personnel turbulence with which the command was afflicted because of our involvement in Vietnam. In the late '60s, most companies were commanded by second lieutenants who remained in command only five to six months. The entire company would turnover within a 12-month period. Effective leadership at the company level practically ceased to exist.

After normal duty hours, when the officers and NCOs began to stop by their clubs or go across the street to be with their families in their drab government quarters, the criminal element took over in the barracks. Coping with such problems would test the most seasoned commander, but from 1967 to 1971 some companies had only one officer and some young lieutenants had to try to command two companies at the same time. It was the inexperienced leading the unwilling. In a few cases, there were young officers who had used ROTC as a means of delaying active service. Some of them had become radicalized and actively fanned the aspirations of the dissenters found in the ranks.

In the pre–Vietnam Army in Europe, the major preoccupation was how to improve training. But during and after the Vietnam War, personnel problems became so acute that training had to give way to attempts to deal with lack of discipline, racial problems, drugs and alcohol, and a host of social problems that afflicted not only the troops in the barracks but the dependents living in the American ghettos as well. Commanders found themselves sinking in a morass of social problems ranging from child abuse to adultery. The lack of meaningful training and work and the social problems were symbiotic. Senior NCOs eligible for retirement would turn down choice jobs in Europe and retire rather than bring their high school-age children to Europe. The shortage of high schools in Germany made it necessary to send some high schoolers to board in Frankfurt and Munich. Prostitution was not uncommon in the larger German cities and some young American girls were making the competition tough on the German regulars. The yellow American school buses that brought the American children home on Fridays often carried the drugs that were to last the troops in the barracks for the next week.

By l972, the demands of Vietnam had been reduced dramatically but the personnel picture in EUCOM was slow to brighten. There was reluctance by some career officers to take commands in Europe. The stakes were high because failure in command could mean eventual release from a shrinking postwar Army. The Army was slow to recognize that much of the problem was systemic and that EUCOM had decayed to the point that successful command was just not possible. One had to do the best one could and hope that the next higher commander would give credit for trying. Unfortunately for some, command in Europe became a career graveyard. Commanders who tried to create interesting training scenarios through adventure training in which the soldiers might succeed or fail were considered too innovative at a time when any kind of failure was the career kiss of death.

For the United States Air Force in Europe, the problems were less acute. As is usually the case, the Air Force, which became independent of the Army in 1947, had much newer barracks, quarters, and facilities than did the Army. According to General Theodore R. Milton, USAF, European duty was a pleasant relief for pilots and aircrew members. It was a chance to be with their families in a generally pleasant environment. Although aircraft spare parts had been in short supply during the war, the Air Force in Europe had been able to maintain an acceptable availability rate for its aircraft and enough flying was permitted to keep everyone from being bored. With a much higher ratio of officer's and NCOs to junior airmen, the social problems of the Air Force were considerably less than that of the Army.

The United States Navy in Europe, on the other hand, had a few more problems than the Air Force, but less than the Army. According to Vice Admiral William P. Mack, the Vietnam War caused the ships of the Pacific Fleet to have longer deployment times. This did not mean that the number of ships assigned to the Sixth U.S. Fleet in the Mediterranean or that the CINCLANT ships in the Atlantic were reduced in number so much as it meant that sea duty tours were extended for everyone. The United States has a commitment to sail a minimum number of ships in support of NATO, so with a good part of the Navy serving extended deployments in the South China Sea, it meant more sea duty for everyone. Long deployments meant lots of hours of hard work and months of separation from loved ones. There were more rapid turnovers of personnel, proficiency dropped, and when ships were not taken care of properly, they began to have mechanical problems that in the end resulted in more work for everyone on board. The long deployments took their toll of experienced officers and petty officers who, having served their time in the combat zone, thought better of a Navy career and elected not to ship over. The same sort of downward spiral that had hit the Army hit the Navy until the Navy's onboard societal problems called for a drastic overhaul of its personnel policies.

The Navy tried to put a quick fix on its personnel problems by installing people-oriented Admiral Elmo Zumwalt as its Chief of Naval Operations. Admiral Zumwalt did much to reach out to the disaffected sailors and tried to make their lives more bearable both ashore and afloat, but he often went around the chain of command to do so and alienated a number of crusty old admirals, senior officers, and petty officers. Indeed, there was a need to treat the ordinary sailor with more dignity and respect and to remove several irritants that could easily be eliminated without a loss of discipline. Historically, the Navy relied upon the draft to scare enough men with the prospect of being conscripted into the Army to fill its berths. However, with the end of the draft, the Navy had to find other ways to attract men to a life lived partially at sea.

In 1972, the effects of the Vietnam War were still being felt through the United States Army. In July, a study group under the leadership of Major General Herbert G. Sparrow was sent out to make a worldwide survey of the Army's personnel problems. His findings were shocking. The Army had grown overnight to meet the demands of the Vietnam War. Thus, instant leaders had been created that did not have the "requisite leaven of knowledge and experience." The problem was compounded when, in mid–1970, the Army began an accelerated phase-down from a strength of 1,500,000 to half of that in two years. Therefore, an Army experiencing severe personnel turbulence problems to meet the needs of a war found itself in worse condition in trying to cover the most important jobs with experienced people, while the Army cut itself in half. Unable to grasp the true nature of the problem, the Army in search of solutions, made many changes that did not have their intended effect but merely added to the confusion. General Sparrow, an officer known to never pull his punches, reported to the Army Chief of Staff:

> The posture of the U.S. Army in the Summer of 1972 was affected also by (1) the unrest of the younger elements of a "permissive" American society; by (2) the continuing disparagement of "the military by the news media and by leading public figures"; and by (3) steps taken to rid the Army of its so-called "Mickey Mouse" image in order to adapt to the time and to attract volunteers. Drug problems, racial incidents, demonstrations and other factors combined with the deep sense of frustration stemming from a war which many felt the military was not permitted to win. These circumstances in combination reacted severely upon the discipline, pride and motivation of the Army. Observable effects:
>
>   a. At many units/installations—a hangdog, slovenly Army (in terms of external manifestations: bearing and appearance);
>
>   b. An Army many of whose Company Commanders were heavily involved in disciplinary actions such as Company punishments, courts and boards. (The percentage of Soldiers receiving Honorable Discharges dropped from 95.8 percent in FY 70 to 89.5 percent in FY 72.)
>
>   c. A widespread, insidious and damaging "I could care less!" attitude which infected the administrative elements as well as others, thus contributing to a vicious circle: poor service to the troops, and "I want out!"

At the root of the crisis in EUCOM was the lack of experience of those left to mind the store in Europe while the war was being fought in Southeast Asia. It was not that they were bad leaders; it was simply that the Vietnam

War exacerbated a number of social problems. As General Michael S. Davison, who commanded the United States Army, Europe in the early 1970s, said: "The drug, race, and disciplinary problems in U.S. Army, Europe, related both to the leadership crisis and to the general unrest of American society. In my view, however, the former was the root of the problem, the latter a major contributing factor." Regardless of the primary cause, the decline of EUCOM brought the United States perilously close to being an ineffective component of the North Atlantic community. Ironically, the investment of men and money in Southeast Asia to preserve the credibility of our system of alliances endangered NATO, the cornerstone of postwar American foreign policy.

Considering the state of readiness of EUCOM during most of the Vietnam War, one might wonder why the Soviets did not attack Western Europe when the major forces of NATO were in such disarray. Perhaps it was fear of nuclear war with the United States and then again, the price the United States was paying around the world for its policies in Southeast Asia must have been a source of great satisfaction to the Soviets. So much so that they may have been content to see the United States continue to weaken itself in Southeast Asia. Proxy war has much to commend it—especially when all it costs is some, for the most part, unsophisticated military equipment. According to Leninist theory, the seeds of capitalism's destruction are sown within. Given a chance, this one of Lenin's theories that might turn out to be correct.

Limited Means, Limited Time and Limited Will

The political decision not to mobilize eventually set the upper limit of United States effort at a level too low to defeat the enemy and internal political pressures set a time limit on the struggle too short to cause the enemy to desist. By the time the North Vietnamese made the error of Tet 1968 and offered the United States an unexpected chance to gain the initiative, there was insufficient will to exploit the opportunity presented because the event was reported incorrectly and because President Johnson was afraid the public would not support the mobilization necessary to do so.

In retrospect, one could say that commander, U.S. Military Assistance Command, Vietnam was a job with little to recommend it. Certainly, no one in his right mind would have taken on such a responsibility if the above conditions and circumstances had been known in advance as part of the job description.

It is said that if labor pains were understood in advance that we might be extinct by now. The question is: Will the United States repeat these same mistakes or variations thereof elsewhere? Hopefully not, but it is of little comfort to note that the mind has marvelous ways of forgetting the unpleasant. That some of us have brothers and sisters suggests that mothers can forget the pain of childbirth.

We may forget the pains and mistakes of Vietnam as well. If there is a next time, and unfortunately there always seems to be, one would hope that the United States will develop sound military aims and provide the means to accomplish them under favorable conditions. When the ends are faulty, they not only preordain the failure of the policy but they also extract a heavy price from the means. In warfare, the military is the major means used by the state. In Vietnam, the American military found itself tasked not to win and not to be defeated. The impact of this dilemma upon the American military and especially upon the United States Army was profound. It revealed the diminished influence of the military upon foreign policy. It also revealed the existence of a number of cracks in the foundation of the Army. If the Army is but a reflection of the society it defends, then the unrest of 1960s and 1970s would suggest that America society had larger problems than its failure to stem the tide of Communism in the post-colonial backwaters of Southeast Asia.

VII

Conduct Unbecoming

The Army isn't what it used to be ... as a matter of fact,
it never was.

—old Army saying

The above saying is a simple formulation of a phenomenon described more elegantly by Sir Lewis Namier, who in 1942 said that "one would expect people to remember the past and to imagine the future. But, in fact, when discoursing or writing about history, they imagine it in terms of their own experience, and when trying to gauge the future, they cite supposed analogies from the past: till, by a double process of repetition, they imagine the past and remember the future."

This phenomenon or what might be termed the "Namier Effect," is familiar, in one form or another, to historians. It is often encountered in interviews and is a special hazard when dealing with oral history. Nevertheless, in trying to assess the impact of the Vietnam era upon the military, in general, and upon the Army, in particular, (with a view toward determining the relevance of those effects upon the military's credibility in the foreign policy formulation process), it is useful to try to gain some idea of what the Army was like or perceived to be like just prior to the Vietnam War.

The late 1950s were lean years for the Army in terms of dollars, but spiritually and professionally the Army was quite robust. The Korean War receded just far enough into the past so its mistakes had been transformed by the Namier Effect. The good lessons learned had been written on tablets of stone by the schools operated by each of the Army's branches. The Korean War, although not won in the traditional sense of the preceding wars, had at least stopped the communist aggression. The *status quo ante-bellum* had been restored.

The Korean War produced its share of heroes who charged against strongly held enemy positions. Overall, the leaders had been good and had taken care of their men. The only clouds upon the war had been the relief of General MacArthur and the fact that large numbers of Americans died after the truce negotiations began.

In those halcyon pre–Vietnam days, there were some top-notch veteran NCOs and officers—men with well-deserved ribbons on their chests. These were men with lines in their faces who had squinted out into the night to detect the next frenzied charge of Red Chinese. They had some war stories to tell and the young soldiers listened. They were listening to men who had faced a dangerous enemy and won. One had to admire the men who had fought and survived on Pork Chop Hill, Heartbreak Ridge, and in the Iron Triangle.

The Army was a draftee one. It depended on a steady supply of mom's apple pie young men who, more or less, represented a cross section of young American manhood. The work ethic was still strong across America and the vast majority of draftees took soldiering seriously during their hitch. A few conscripts stayed on to become "RA" or Regular Army, but most of them looked upon their two-year conscription as a duty to be completed and, without rancor, passed back into the mainstream of civilian life. For most of them, "the Army was a good experience, but I wouldn't want to do it again."

In the Cold War, there was a sense of holy mission. The world was clearly a dangerous place even as America prospered as never before. The communist threat gave no sign of letting up and some of the best scholars in academe were giving their talents to conceive of ways that the Western democracies might prevail or at least maintain the status quo. If one did not go to a service academy, ROTC was the "thing to do" for young men who could afford college or who would work their way through. A Regular Army career was attractive to many college-educated young men who sensed the danger of the Cold War and who did not want to become the man in the gray flannel suit.

The communist threat attracted some splendid young officers to the colors. The draft was providing some fine young enlisted men to balance the sometimes not-so-fine volunteers who could not find better paying jobs in an economy that then was booming. At $78 per month for the buck private and $222.50 per month for the second lieutenant, the pay was not good, but there were certain intangibles. There were no signs on lawns saying, SOLDIERS AND DOGS KEEP OFF. The public was mindful of the communist threat and the need to have a certain amount of defense—a fact that made the off-duty serviceman not ashamed to wear his uniform to town. Indeed, most servicemen and their parents were happy when the hometown newspaper printed their pictures along with a press release from the military saying that he or she had just graduated from basic training or boot camp.

When a crisis arose in Lebanon, the United States went ashore and almost as quickly as it began it was over. There was a scare in the Far East when the Chinese communists threatened the tiny offshore islands of Quemoy, Matsu, and Amoy. The United States Seventh Fleet put on a show of force and the United States Air Force gave the Nationalist Chinese Air Force a few Sidewinder missiles that routed the Red Chinese MiG fighters that ventured out to sea. When the Russians caused the Autobahn leading from West Germany to Berlin to be blocked, a tough, well-trained United States Seventh Army moved a Task Force to the inter-zonal border and the roadblocks were taken down.

Perhaps this description of the Army's "good old pre–Vietnam days" suffers from the Namier Effect, but it is surely more accurate than any future that could have imagined by military personnel at the beginning of the 1960s. Who would believe that by and just after the turn of the next decade:

- That a major general, the provost marshal of the Army, would be tried and convicted of obtaining confiscated handguns from civilian police departments for free and selling them for personal profit to a private gun dealer in North Carolina?
- That the Army's top enlisted soldier and several other high-ranking NCOs would be tried and convicted for operating a worldwide racket skimming millions of dollars from the operations of officer, NCO, and service clubs?
- That a major general, when he commanded a division in Germany, was an important protector of the so-called "NCO Mafia" behind the club scandals (and personally profited from them); and later, in retirement, headed a construction firm in Vietnam that was so corrupt that its acronym, PA&E, was dubbed "Promises, Alibis, and Excuses" by the troops the construction firm was supposed to support?
- That a brigadier general responsible for the operation of all the post exchanges and clubs in Vietnam would be tried and convicted for aiding and abetting the "NCO Mafia" to rob the clubs and exchanges and to skim millions of dollars from the

operation of bordellos, black market dealings, and numerous kickback schemes?

- That a United States Army second lieutenant would direct and participate in the murder of between 175 and 400 noncombatant Vietnamese men, women, and children at the two hamlets of Son My (known as My Lai)?
- That as the result of a thorough and detailed investigation, the major general in charge of the United States Military Academy at West Point would be relieved and demoted for his role in covering up the My Lai Massacre?
- That junior enlisted men in Vietnam would kill and attempt to kill their officers and senior NCO by "fragging" them with hand grenades and other explosive devices?
- That the use of mind-altering chemicals (drugs and alcohol) would become a major problem within the Armed Forces?
- That the Armed Services which had been first to begin racial integration and first to begin to provide a measure of equal opportunity to minority members would be shaken by racial riots and discord?
- That the first black general to command a division would be caught by the District of Columbia Revenue Service for failing to file his income taxes?
- That a United States Navy ship, the USS *Pueblo*, would be seized by communist forces in international waters and give up without a fight?
- That during air combat operations over North Vietnam a race riot would break out on the USS *Kitty Hawk.*
- That an Air Force general would be relieved for carrying on a secret air war in Southeast Asia which was obviously known to the Joint Chiefs of Staff?
- That the prisoners in an Army stockade would mutiny and that when the commanding general in charge attempted to court-martial them, he would not be backed by his civilian superiors?
- That the Army would attempt a major reform to eliminate "Mickey Mouse" elements in order to attract on all-volunteer force, and that the effort would be sabotaged, in part, by reactionary senior officers and NCOs?
- That several highly decorated and supposedly "up and coming" Army officers would resign or retire and write exposes of alleged

109

"careerism," "ticket-punching," and ethical lapses within the officer corps?

- That 33 of the Army's presumably most outstanding young officers would resign while assigned as faculty as the United States Military Academy?
- That Lieutenant General William Peers would attach a memo to his report on the My Lai Massacre suggesting to the Army chief of staff that a major study should be made of the professional and moral climate of the Army—a memo that "shook [General Westmoreland] to the core?"
- That the United States Army War College would conduct the study suggested by General Peers and ordered by General Westmoreland and that the results would be so damning of the officer corps that the report's first recommendation: "That it be given the widest possible dissemination" was given only lip service?

The Army War College Professionalism Study of 1970

The United States Army War College Professionalism Study of 1970 came as a thunderbolt to the senior leaders of the Army. The study group interrogated 450 officers ranging in rank from lieutenant to general who described their typical fellow officer as

> an ambitious, transitory commander—marginally skilled in the complexities of his duties—engulfed in producing statistical results, fearful of personal failure, too busy to talk with or listen to subordinates, and determined to submit acceptable optimistic reports which reflect faultless completion of a variety of tasks at the expense of the sweat and frustration of his subordinates.

This report, too damaging to be released, coming on top of a series of exposes of criminal acts and derelictions of duty by the officer corps and by a few NCOs, immediately raised the question of how the supposed guardians of duty-honor-country could allow such a condition to come about?

The first answer that comes to mind is to say that war brings out the best and the worst in people. That may be so, but armies are supposed to exist for wartime operations. The supposed purpose of military training and indoctrination is to steel men and units physically and morally against the crucible of war so that they can carry out the aims of policy while adhering to the code of duty-honor-country.

The next answer would be to say that the Army is a reflection of society and that in the 1960s the general society experienced a period of upheaval manifested by permissive sexual attitudes, reduced church attendance, disrespect for law and order, increased use of drugs and alcohol, civil disobedience, and violent dissent against the United States' foreign and domestic policies.

While that argument has a certain appeal, the general unrest was due in large measure to an anomalous demographic situation. During the 1960s, the United States experienced the largest number of citizens in the 17 to 23-year old age bracket in its history. This is the age group that produces more crime and rebellion than any other. But when this youth bubble on the population graph passed into the 1970s, the turmoil it had produced in the 1960s ebbed only slightly. Because the Army's major business has been the reception, training, and indoctrination of masses of people in just that age group, the Army should have done considerably better in dealing with the unrest of the 1960s than it did. The reason the Army did so poorly what it had done well before is because it was not prepared professionally, morally, or ethically for either the Vietnam War or for the influx of young people from the troubled general society.

The cause of this unpreparedness is manifold. It began in World War II with a rapid promotion from lieutenant to colonel of the officers who would be the general officers of the Army on the eve of the Vietnam War. This is not to say that anything was particularly wrong with those officers professionally or ethically, but it should be recognized that they served only briefly as platoon leaders and as company commanders, and mostly in combat—rather than garrison training situations. In addition, the problems of peacetime command, while less dangerous, are in many ways more demanding and complex than those faced in combat. With the drastic reduction in size of the Army immediately after World War II, there were few platoons to lead or companies to command or to even observe. Thus, those very young colonels were too senior to serve with troops and there were very few troop units with which to serve. These officers had to staff the schools and the higher headquarters that remained in existence as a cadre against the need for another Army expansion. Thus elevated, they were also isolated from many of the realities of Army life in the combat companies, troops, and batteries. As a result, they would know very little about the professional perceptions of the generations of officers under them who would be the focus of the studies that culminated in the Army War College Professionalism Study of 1970.

The generals who would lead the Army at the start of the Vietnam era graduated from the U.S. Military Academy in the middle and late 1930s. When they entered the Army, their peers, who were non-academy graduates, provided little competition for the West Pointers. Many of the reserve officers on active duty and the few non-academy Regular Army officers had private incomes that enabled them to devote considerable attention to polo and social life. By and large the West Pointers depended upon soldiering for their income and thus took it more seriously than did their socialite fellow officers. When war came, and with it the chance for rapid promotion, the top spots went to the West Pointers.

But when General Harold K. Johnson was Army chief of staff, the number of non–West Point generals increased considerably. This was due to the increased quality of the ROTC and OCS officers remaining on active duty following World War II.

During the Vietnam War, the Army served under three different chiefs of staff: Harold K. Johnson, William C. Westmoreland, and Creighton Abrams. It would be difficult indeed to make the case that any one of these three officers suffered any faults of character. Their only real handicaps were those that resulted from rapid promotion and its resulting isolation.

General Harold K. Johnson was on the Bataan death march. He survived the cruelest hardships in good measure due to his deep Christian beliefs. Although he did not come out of the war as senior as did Westmoreland and Abrams, he had little opportunity for postwar troop duty, because in order to allow him to catch up with his peers who had not been imprisoned, the Army kept him going from service school to service school. As a lieutenant colonel, he commanded a half-strength infantry battalion that was literally thrown into the breach in Korea. He saw some exceedingly hard infantry fighting in Korea. His final troop assignment was twenty months as an assistant division commander in Europe.

To Johnson, the good Christian did not need to shout or be assertive. His calling was to work diligently and quietly at his profession. He was a team player who could see the other fellow's point of view. He was not mean, nor petty, nor vindictive. He did not climb to high rank by leaving cleat marks on the backs of his peers. He gratefully accepted any amount of work given him by his superiors and did it to the best of his considerable abilities. He accepted reverses as God's will and continued to do his best. He was doing just that in the backbreaking job of deputy chief of staff for operations when he was selected over 42 more senior general officers to replace General Earle Wheeler as Army chief of staff.

No one has ever questioned his integrity or strict adherence to the highest standards of personal and official conduct, nor did he tolerate less from those around him. The only criticism heard about General Johnson was that he was too uncritical of the management methods imposed by Secretary of Defense McNamara. General Johnson had just the qualities the secretary wanted. He was intelligent, able, hardworking, and not given to making political end runs to Congress.

General William C. Westmoreland was another example of an officer whose personal and professional life was lived in accordance with the highest standards. He always had all the virtues of the All-American boy and no apparent vices. If one hears him criticized it is for being too willing to believe the best about his fellow man and for being too optimistic about the course of the future.

General Creighton Abrams, who liked cigars, whiskey, and Patton-esque language, was widely respected as a "soldier's soldier," marked by the courage of his convictions and having both the willingness and the skill to stand up to his (civilian) superiors on issues of moment to the Army. He was not one to temporize over ethical matters. He was known as an officer of uncompromising integrity.

If the men at the top of the Army during the Vietnam era were so sterling how then did the officer corps become the career-oriented, ticket-punching, false-reporting body described in the Army War College Professionalism Study of 1970? Brigadier General George D. Eggers, Jr., USA (Ret.) suggests that

> our Chiefs of Staff during the late sixties and early seventies did not preach and practice integrity in a manner that discouraged self-seeking within the officer corps. Their time and energies were devoted principally to coping with the immediate and vexatious problems at the Pentagon level: the day-to-day conduct of the war in Southeast Asia, their civilian superior's lack of confidence in the ability of the military to manage that conflict.

Trying to wage an unpopular war without a formal declaration of war was a Herculean task. Given the tremendous responsibilities of raising a fighting force without the reserve structure designed to support it, one might understand why the service chiefs might not see the need to spend much time stressing the values supposedly already solidly built into the officer corps. They had been raised in the environment of duty-honor-country and service before self. Unfortunately, as four-star flag officers, they were now too senior, too isolated, too beset by civilian attack, and too busy to realize that the ethnological foundations of the forces they had to rely on were rotting away.

Every Soldier a Field Marshal

Although the officers at the top were not the cause of the decay, they were certainly among the victims. They were victims of their own high rank and of the machinations of those younger officers under them who made it their business to present their commands and activities in the best possible light to the next higher headquarters. Senior officers are extremely busy people. When they go out to the field to see what is going on, it is easy for lower commanders and their staffs to construct itineraries that keep the senior visitors moving rapidly and that focus attention upon what is going well at the expense or what is going wrong. Consequently, in a hierarchical organization, it is almost impossible to pierce the protective barriers erected by each subordinate headquarters if the officials in charge of those headquarters are motivated to minimize the actual in favor of the desired but nonexistent ideal.

What brought about this motivation to convince each higher headquarters that all tasks were being faultlessly completed? Human nature in part, but human nature twisted by the intense competition among the talented officers who entered the Army during the Cold War. Added to that was the setting of false goals and unrealistic expectations by the service academies and by the individual branches of the Army.

Prior to World War II, the Army was quite small. If one attained the rank of lieutenant colonel or colonel one was deemed successful. The pre–World War II Army had only a handful of general officer billets and with the expansion of the Army during the Cold War there came to be approximately 500 general officer billets. Somehow, there grew the expectation that all officers should strive to attain a general's star. A letter from General Andrew Goodpaster who served as superintendent at West Point (recalled from retirement in the wake of an extensive honor code scandal), to General Bruce C. Clarke, USA (Ret.) illustrates this point:

> the idea has been fostered that if a man does not become a general—and a senior general at that—that his life as an officer will have been wasted and that he is a failure.... I would try to break the syndrome that says every officer must be a general if he is going to succeed.

VII. Conduct Unbecoming

I am spending a good deal of thought on trying to define the line between simulative, healthy competition and corruptive, damaging competition, recognizing that the first is an element in the kind of pride that makes fine soldiers while the second can be ruinous to the quality and integrity of an outfit.

Therefore, if star rank is the accepted goal, one could not afford just to be promoted on time. Indeed, one or two accelerated or "below the promotion zone," or "deep selection" promotions would have to be attained.

In the pre–World War II Army, where once foreign or United States tactics and organization or even polo scores had dominated on- and off-duty conversation, the conversation in the growing Cold War Army tended to center upon the results of the latest promotion board. Individual officers spent vast amounts of time studying the biographies of those selected to higher rank in order to determine the assignments the selectees had held to divine the stepping-stones to promotion.

Such studies were not confined to a few ambitious officers. The personnel managers in each of the Army's separate branches made detailed analyses of promotion board results and published their findings to the members of their branch. Not only did the officers become locked in a keen competition for higher rank, but so did the separate branches—each determined to place more of its officers on the next promotion list than the other branches.

In a society which claims to revere competition, one might ask, what is wrong with officers striving so mightily to get ahead? An excellent analysis of this problem is provided by a staff paper that staffers working on the Modern Volunteer Army (MVA) Project promoted to get the Army staff to carry out the reforms recommended by the Army War College Professionalism Study:

The historical charter of the competitive attitude in the Army is founded on the "playing fields of Eton," and upon General Douglas MacArthur's "fields of friendly strife." In the sense that this competitive attitude fosters a will to persevere in the face of any adversity, then the attitude is clearly an asset. However, this spirit is most often manifested as a will to win, and implies that adversity was overcome by the winner. Missing in this deification of "winning" is the clear understanding and universal acceptance of the fact that the will to win must be anchored upon the requirement to "do it right." (In this case, "do it right" means that one must be tactically and technically proficient and understand the moral obligation to abide by rules.)

The will to win, when it combines both the perseverance in the face of adversity and the determination to do it right, is a critical necessity to the rifle company commander who leads the final assault with grenades and bayonets, to the lead tank commander in the breakthrough, to the artilleryman in the counter battery mission, or to the medical evacuation pilot coming into a hot pickup zone. This is exactly what MacArthur intended to instill in the mind and behavioral patterns of future officers.

However, when the analogy is extended to each and every field of endeavor, in war and peace, for all units of a command, then the "will to win" ethic loses many of the virtues of do it right and perseverance. The extended requirement to demonstrate the will to win, falls victim to the assumption that the winner did all of this, and the "finish first" aspect prevails as the sole survivor.

Rather than being an overall benefit to the Army, this finish first fixation is actually counterproductive to honest mission accomplishment.

Indeed, honesty was the essential element the officer corps had lost as it approached the Vietnam Era. In a memorandum, one of the senior members of the Modern Volunteer Army staff summed up the thrust of the Army War College Professionalism Study in one sentence: "The central issue surfaced in the AWC Professional Study is the pressure in our system which results in promotion-centered dishonesty." The up or out policy operated to demand faultless perfection but in fact received only a presentation of statistics—manipulated if necessary—to indicate zero defects.

The idea that the central motivation for the officer corps was promotion came as a shock to General Westmoreland, the officer who commissioned the study. The initial reaction of the Army staff was opposition to the findings of the study. The conditions reported were denied or were explained away as being the aberrational result of a small improperly selected sample. One lieutenant general told General Westmoreland that the AWC study was only an account of misfits and malcontents, attempting to rationalize their own failures. However, Lieutenant General William E. DePuy contested this alibi by pointing out that this could hardly be the case because many of the officers interviewed in the course of the study were students at the Army War College who could hardly be called misfits or failures.

The genesis of this promotion-centered dishonesty was found by the AWC study to be putting promotion before service. As a result of this unending quest for early promotion, many officers directed their loyalty only upward, reported only favorable results, sought exposure to higher officers, and sought a variety of jobs in order to get the right punches in their ticket to stardom. This rapid shift from one job to another precluded their knowing their men or establishing mutual trust and confidence with them.

Due, in part to the McNamara management system, centralized

control resulted in detailed status reporting and reliance upon statistics instead of a professional feel for the actual status of units. The Army became fixated upon measurable trivia, which only measured short-term results. Consequently, there was little awareness of deep, long-term, non-quantifiable issues and trends within the Army. With those operating the reporting system determined to reflect zero defects in a wide variety of tasks, superiors at each higher echelon of command became hopelessly misinformed about the true condition of the Army.

These findings might not be all that important if they had to do with the internal state of the management of a private corporation; however, this report indicted those charged with the defense of the nation. In assessing what would happen if the Army failed to correct itself, the AWC Study went on to say:

- It is not unreasonable to state as consequences of the present climate;
- It is conducive to self-deception because it fosters the production of inaccurate information;
- It impacts on the long-term ability of the Army to fight and win because it frustrates young, idealistic, energetic officers who leave the service and are replaced by those who will tolerate if not condone ethical imperfection;
- It is corrosive of the Army's image because it falls short of the traditional idealistic code of the soldier;
- A code which is the key to the soldier's acceptance by a modern free society;
- It lowers the credibility of our top military leaders because it shields them from essential bad news; it stifles initiative, innovation, and humility because it demands perfection or the pose of perfection at every turn;
- It downgrades technical competence by rewarding instead trivial, measurable, quota-filling accomplishments; and,
- It eventually squeezes much of the inner satisfaction and personal enjoyment out of being an officer.

However, despite the urgency of the need for reform, the AWC study, although not classified in the sense of security information, was placed on a "close hold" status. It was, however, covered in the weekly summary that goes out to senior commanders and staffs. At the November 1970 Chief of Staff Commanders' Conference, it was briefed to the commanders of the

Army major commands. Their general reaction was very much like that of the Army staff—it ranged from disbelief to outrage.

The AWC study was a damning indictment of them and what they were doing worldwide. The conditions it identified, when not corrected, were major causes of the Army's failure to attract and *retain* capable volunteers.

The Deceived Leading the Deceivers

> The Moving Finger writes; and, having writ,
> Moves on: nor all thy Piety nor Wit
> Shall lure it back to cancel half a line,
> Nor all thy tears wash out a word of it.
> —Taken from *The Rubaiyat* by Omar Khayyam

The casualties of this upward scramble for promotion were the troops who had to endure a rapid turnover of commanders as each officer tried his hand at a short span of command in order to get his ticket punched as a commander prior to a short stint at whatever staff job was in vogue. After each promotion board, a new fad wave was generated toward this field or that. As a result, the troops were not only bewildered by a carousel of changing policies but the ticket-punchers themselves came to know very little about many things.

Ultimately, it became almost impossible to tell not only the true status of the readiness of the units in the Army, but almost to tell much about the qualities and the performance of those in charge of running it. The deceived were leading the deceivers.

Each echelon, in turn, put the best face upon what it received from below and passed it up to the next higher echelon. Finally, there was little relevance between the reports that reached the top and the true state of the Army's ability or inability to move, shoot, communicate, and command.

How then could the Army have done as well as it did in the actual fighting in Vietnam? The answer lies in the nature of actual combat. Danger mutually faced by young men generates its own ethic. Even though some middle echelon commanders—battalion and brigade—might feel it necessary to lie to higher headquarters about statistically presented results internally—within the fire team, squad, platoon and company—hostile fire produces an internal ethic that demands absolute honesty and integrity in assessing the threat and what to do about it. To men faced with the real-world problem of staying alive, promotion becomes an abstraction.

This internal ethic may also explain the magnificent performance of the American prisoners of war held by the North Vietnamese. This subject is beyond the scope of this book, but some facets of the POW story are relevant. For example, if one compares the conduct of American POWs in North Korean prison camps with that of those held in the Hanoi Hilton and other camps in North Vietnam, one would conclude that there has been a rise rather than a decline in the moral climate of the officer corps. However, the demographics of the two POW populations are dramatically dissimilar. Our Korean War POWs were predominantly young, inexperienced, partly educated Army troops without any training or indoctrination against the rigors they would face. After the Korean War, their serious lack of morale and resistance prompted the establishment of a Code of Conduct. The POW population in North Vietnam was predominantly Air Force, Navy, and Marine pilots with considerable formal education, active service, and indoctrination in the Code of Conduct to include some rigorous training on how to endure and resist in the POW environment. Thus, comparing the two POW experiences is comparing apples to oranges.

Promotion-centered dishonesty no doubt operated to some degree in all the services, but as stated earlier, the hazards of flight do not permit one to take many liberties with the facts. Launching, flying, and recovering airplanes takes place in an environment governed by immutable laws the violation of which can rarely be covered over by false or optimistic reports. Conversely, the true ability of ground combat forces to accomplish their mission is impossible to assess accurately in peacetime. A truly realistic assessment of the Army's ability to engage in ground combat cannot be made unless the nation is willing to accept the actual personnel and equipment losses that would be the certain result of a field maneuver that closely approximated actual combat. The public has never permitted it before, and it is highly unlikely that it ever will. Thus, because accurate measurements in peacetime of the Army's ability to accomplish many of its wartime missions are not made, there must be a great deal of latitude for subjective judgment. But when the subjective judgment of experienced officers is replaced by statistics which quantify in isolation that which can be quantified, the opportunities for statistical manipulation are considerable. It is this environment that makes the Army more prone to the affliction of promotion-centered dishonesty.

The Joint Chiefs of Staff

Other major casualties of promotion-centered dishonesty were the flag officers who headed the armed services and sat as members of the Joint Chiefs of Staff. The focal point of the promotion-corrupted reporting system was the Pentagon. Thus, those charged with the operation of United States forces deployed at home and around the periphery of the Sino Soviet land mass were doing so from faulty data.

In the Kennedy Administration there had been concern that the Joint Chiefs of Staff really did not know what they were talking about. This concern went beyond the debate over quantifiable data versus professional judgment and "feel." It stemmed from the fact that no matter how well the senior officers had served in World War II or Korea, no matter how sterling were their characters they were serving in splendid isolation from the realities of the forces whose professional ethos and competence were being eroded by the unremitting pressures to reflect faultless performance of a variety of tasks. The demands of McNamara for more and more quantifiable data exacerbated this condition.

Although the major weight of the evidence presented indicts the Army officer corps there is also evidence that the other armed services have been affected by the same pressures that affected the Army. Navy Captain Robert H. Smith, writing in the prestigious *U.S. Naval Institute Proceedings* in March 1971, focused upon the question of the credibility of the leadership of the Navy when he wrote that "no one has been long in the Pentagon without hearing the familiar, disgusted lament, 'We've lied to 'em so often that now they don't believe a word we say.' ... So long as the system in which an officer matures is one that esteems the juggler of figures, and rewards men who can 'sell' shaky programs over a man who stubbornly insists that a bad one be killed, then we will still be in trouble."

The Air Force had its share of credibility problems as well. For one thing, it could not quit deceiving itself about the capabilities of airpower. Despite overwhelming historical evidence to the contrary in World War II, Korea, and then Vietnam, the leadership of the Air Force still depicted airpower as a military panacea.

Air power is, thus far, a proven deterrent of thermonuclear war and, assuming it has air superiority or can gain it, has been useful in the support of ground operations. But it has yet, with the possible exception of the Kosovo operation, to end a war by itself by destroying an enemy's ability to wage war or by interdicting the enemy's ability to supply his troops on the battlefield. *The Pentagon Papers* are the record of a running battle between the secretary of defense and his staff and the air staff over this very issue. A little less hyperbole on the part of the Air Force planners might not have changed the outcome of the war, but it would have enhanced the credibility of the Air Force. Commenting on this, Air Force General Theodore R. Milton said, "The military was by no means blameless in all this. There was an awful lot of parochialism in the military in the Vietnam years. It suddenly became clear to everybody in every service that this is how you got money and new weapons, built your force structure and got promotions and everything else. They didn't think much of the way the civilians were running it, but since that was the way it was going to be run, everybody better get aboard."

Institutional self-interest and the faulty data upon which military advice was relying upon had a greater and more tragic impact than was readily apparent. It eroded the credibility of the military leaders in all areas. If there is a bottom-line expectation of professionals, it is that they know what they are talking about. If the military leadership had inaccurate facts on the readiness of its men and equipment by implication their judgment and feel for grand and military strategy would be equally faulty. The possession of faulty data about the condition of the military in a micro context reflected unfavorably upon the ability of the military to advise effectively about the employment and operation of military forces in a macro context.

This is not to say that the service chiefs were not important to the effort in Vietnam. They were terribly important. They had to raise and train the forces that were used to man the unified and specified commands worldwide. They had to provide the forces that fought so well in Vietnam; but as a corporate body charged by law to advise the president, the National Security Council, and the secretary of defense they were not of particular importance. Major United States ground, air, and naval elements had been fighting in Southeast Asia for twenty months before Mr. McNamara felt it was necessary to reply to the repeated attempts of the Joint Chiefs of Staff to get him to endorse their "defeat the enemy" strategy or to just say something one way or the other. According to Dean Rusk, the real decisions about the conduct of the Vietnam War were made at the Tuesday luncheons held at the White House. It was not until the spring of 1967 that the chairman of the Joint Chiefs of Staff was invited to attend those sessions. This enlargement of the decision-making group only came about because, as President Johnson's popularity began to slip, he was accused of not listening to military advice on how to run the war. Finally, when Senator John Stennis of the Armed Services Committee made such a complaint, President Johnson allowed General Wheeler to attend the Tuesday luncheons.

Had General Wheeler been allowed to attend the earlier Tuesday luncheons, he would have been aware that Secretary Rusk, via the Swiss, was giving the North Vietnamese advance notice of when U.S. fighter-bombers would be attacking specific Vietnamese factories. Rusk said this was done to give the North Vietnamese time to send factory workers home before the bombs fell. In Part Six of the Canadian television series "The Ten Thousand Day War, Vietnam, 1945–1975," Secretary Rusk states this in his own words. In that same segment, U.S. Senator William Fulbright says presidential adviser, Walter Rostow, told him why the North Vietnamese were being warned in advance about specific targets and times: to save civilian lives. Apparently, no one in the Johnson White House realized the North Vietnamese would use this advance targeting information to amass anti-aircraft guns around the targets and put their MiG-17s and Chinese-based MiG-21s on high alert. These advanced warnings to the North Vietnamese explain, in large measure, the huge losses of pilots and aircraft experienced by the U.S. Air Force and Navy.

There is probably never a good time for a profession to become corrupted. Tragically, the officer corps of the Army and to some degree the officer corps of the other armed services allowed their professional and moral ethos to be eroded by the activities of some, but not all, of their members. As the United States entered and fought its, fourth major war of the twentieth century, this decline of honor, integrity, and competence within the armed forces could not have come at a worse time.

Johnson's Silver Star

The idea that the Joint Chiefs of Staff or their chairman should have been more effective in convincing the makers of grand strategy to provide a winning strategy plus the means to carry it out and to allow the military to control its own operations is open to challenge. After all, why should we expect men who have been conditioned to say, "Yes, sir!" for their entire professional lives to suddenly suggest, "No, sir. Let us suggest a way to achieve your ends with less cost"?

Perhaps that is too much to expect from modern-day military leaders, but there were civilians in the United States government who did dissent from official policy and were able to get it changed. Townsend Hoopes and Clark Clifford are two examples. Hoopes, as secretary of the Air Force, waged a long but effective campaign to get McNamara to see that the bombing of North Vietnam was not producing the results that McNamara had expected. Due in good measure to Hoopes's efforts, there were bombing pauses, geographical limits, and long halts. Clifford, who started out to be a hawk, made a study of the war after he became secretary of defense and emerged a dove. Clifford maneuvered President Johnson into seeking a negotiated settlement and the beginning of the winding down of the American involvement.

Why were these civilians successful in changing policy to suit their convictions while the Joint Chiefs of Staff were not? Perhaps this is comparing apples and oranges. If that is the case, then it must be deduced that apples are better than oranges and that may be so.

It may be that men like Hoopes and Clifford were more articulate or more skillful in maneuvering on the Washington terrain. It may have been that President Johnson was more impressed with Ivy League background, with private success and wealth than with military academy graduates with no wealth and who lived their entire lives in the cocoon of the military bureaucracy. Perhaps the civilians were more active and more skillful at lining up horses on their side of the debate—a factor important to the president who liked to tally the number of advisers for and against an issue. Or, perhaps, Johnson's suspicions of the military simply allowed the civilians to win by default. Who knows? But it is clear that the Joint Chiefs of Staff, severally and jointly, had little clout with their commander-in-chief. President Johnson probably knew that McNamara's lateral arabesque to the World Bank would please the Joint Chiefs of Staff, but that does not mean that McNamara's transfer was done to placate them.

Clearly Johnson was not a man to make up his mind in a vacuum. He actively sought the opinions of those he trusted and respected. As his longtime aide Bill Moyers said: "President Johnson relies less upon military advice than any president since Wilson." But by the time that President Johnson was more willing to listen to the Joint Chiefs of Staff, it was too late. Public support, drained by the length of the indecisive conflict and by the wholly inaccurate media portrayals of Tet 1968 and thereafter, was gone. By then, there was no apparent choice but to go against his own Texas upbringing and "cut and run."

Compared to Presidents Roosevelt, Truman, Eisenhower, and Kennedy, Lyndon Johnson had little interest in military affairs. Although

President Roosevelt never actually served on active duty, he had a lifelong interest in naval matters. As assistant secretary of the Navy, he loved to stand watches on the bridges of warships and frequently took the helm himself.

President Johnson had no real military experience. He served for eight months as an "instant" lieutenant commander in World War II. He made a 34-day tour of the Pacific as Roosevelt's personal representative. During that time, Congressman Johnson was riding in a military aircraft that was shot at and missed by a Japanese aircraft. When Johnson returned to Washington, he pressed the Navy for an award of the Silver Star, our nation's third-highest award for valor. No one else on that aircraft received any kind of commendation. Johnson's ability to manipulate the Navy probably served to make him distrust the integrity of a system willing to prostitute itself to win the support of a (then) relatively junior congressman. (When the newly retired General Harold K. Johnson took this writer to lunch at the Army-Navy Club in Washington, D.C., General Johnson said, "Every time I saw President Johnson wear that Silver Star lapel pin, it made me want to puke.")

Both Roosevelt and Truman relied heavily on military men to give them military advice. They did not always take it, but they always insisted upon receiving it straight from the admirals and generals. Truman served admirably as a captain of artillery in World War I. Both men knew that military advice and political advice each stemmed from a different set of considerations. When General Patton began to make noises that sounded like foreign policy pronouncements, he was silenced. When MacArthur went even farther, he was fired by Truman. Both Roosevelt and Truman knew the value of professional military men working in their own vineyard. They also knew it was the duty of the president and commander-in-chief to wear two hats. It is the chief executive who must assimilate the sometimes contending inputs he receives and make from them a national strategy that harnesses the capabilities of the nation to the accomplishment of worthwhile and attainable goals and the defense of its vital interests.

Unfortunately for America, a president unskilled in foreign and military affairs, a secretary of defense who was able to pass off systems analysis for military strategy, and a group of non-uniformed defense intellectuals who wanted to experiment with counterinsurgency were able to cow the American military into conducting a war in Asia in violation of almost all the Principles of War. As Nicholas von Hoffman said in *The Washington Post*:

VII. Conduct Unbecoming

If you reflect on it, the behavior of the brass during the Vietnamese war was one of almost touching loyalty to our political institutions.

The crazy civilians ordered them into a war which they weren't allowed to fight as they thought best and, in the ensuing stalemate, they absorbed a home front bombardment of ridicule and anger. Through it all the generals not only gave no thought to rebelling, they hardly ever even grumbled in public.

Fortunately for the United States, the year was not 1941 nor were the stakes as high. The United States was given a painful lesson in Vietnam. Let us hope the lesson will see us through the more vital challenges that are certain to come in a world of expanding demand and shrinking resources.

VIII

One War Too Far

The nation that will insist on drawing a broad line of demarcation between the fighting man and the thinking man is liable to find its fighting done by fools and its thinking done by cowards.
—Sir William Francis Butler, 1838–1910

America's flawed foreign policy toward Southeast Asia and the unsatisfactory way it was pursued by military means in Vietnam was due to the confluence of several factors into a policy stream. First, was the general thrust of the Truman Doctrine and the policy of containment. Second, was the activist tenor of the New Frontier. Third, was the general weakening of the position of the military in the decision-making process which received tremendous acceleration by the appearance of Mr. McNamara and his management methods. Finally, there were a number of errors made by the United States government at home and abroad which provided the impetus for additional steps down a path poorly selected. The overthrow of the Diem Regime in South Vietnam is a case in point. Each new advisory element, each new troop and material commitment to Southeast Asia added to the snowballing involvement. Coming together as they did at the wrong time, they produced the feared "wrong war, at the wrong time, and at the wrong place." Once committed, the United States went about the war the wrong way as well.

Some of the factors mentioned in this brief recapitulation bear more elaboration because they contain many valuable lessons for our country.

The men who made the fateful decisions in Vietnam were not villains. They were simply the products of their times. They were mindful that when decision-makers before them had appeased the aggressor major war had been the result. The experience of the Cold War taught them that resolution in the face of the communist threat was not only a viable policy but perhaps the only policy they should adopt.

However, all policies, no matter how successful, have an outer limit—a point beyond which they either do not apply or beyond which there is not a means to enforce them, or beyond which the risks they encounter are too great. The great test of statesmanship is to know the limits to which a policy can be carried and enforced without running unacceptable risk—the risk of trying to wage a war too far.

In the early 1960s, American was a tremendous military power. The country was vibrant under the youthful John F. Kennedy. Indeed, it was ready to "pay any price, bear any burden, meet any hardships, support any friend, oppose any foe to assure the survival and the success of liberty." But implicit in President Kennedy's exhortation was the assumption that the list of acts we would undertake were only those *necessary* to the survival and success of liberty.

Unfortunately, Kennedy's successor was not adequately trained to know the difference between what was necessary to the survival and success of liberty and what was not. Or, if he did, he felt constrained politically to do more of whatever President Kennedy had been doing.

It would be too pat to say that Johnson was an accidental president who got us into an accidental war. The war was no accident. There is a fundamental difference between accident and error. President Kennedy and his advisers made the first error when they tried to extend the Truman Doctrine beyond the reach of America's political power. For it was one thing to topple President Diem, but it was quite another to put an effective replacement in his place. President Johnson compounded Kennedy's error by trying to save the situation by military means.

President Johnson, of course, was not alone in all of this. There were strategies and doctrines that cried for testing. There were professions and institutions that wanted to play a role in the imposition of the Pax Americana upon Southeast Asia. There were even those who saw personal gain or advancement in the undertaking. Although Southeast Asia was at the outer limit of American political influence, it was not beyond American military capability to have won a military victory over the Viet Cong and the North Vietnamese Armed Forces. However, the Johnson Administration, out of deference to the Sino-Soviet military threat, twisted the Allied military effort in two dimensions—*time* and *space*.

In space, because, as Sir Robert Thompson pointed out, the United States never understood that the outcome of the struggle rested upon a contest for the rear bases of the opposing parties. In time, because as Norman Hannah observed, the United States did not attack the Cambodian and Laotian sanctuaries, mine the North Vietnamese harbors, and begin the strategic bombardment of the enemy base areas until the other dimension—time—had run out. Finally, the American people had experienced too many casualties, too much cost, and too much domestic unrest and inflation. As a consequence of domestic political pressures, the United States agreed to a cease fire that assured the enemy that its rear bases would never be threatened again. Therefore, as Sir Robert Thompson contends, if the outcome of the war depended upon which side would eventually conquer the other's rear bases, the ultimate winner of the war could be predicted with ease.

While all of this is rather clear today, it does not explain why the American military failed to make manifest to President Johnson and his civilian advisers, as the war was being entered, what seems so clear in retrospect. There is plenty of evidence that the military understood what was necessary to win, but the military was never able to get a coherent strategy to win from the Johnson Administration.

Because the civilian authorities, no matter what they said about winning, would only underwrite with adequate means the desist strategy, the win strategy could not succeed. Because the conditions under which the win strategy was undertaken precluded the destruction of the enemy's base areas, the win strategy could not succeed. For the desist strategy to succeed, the American people would have to be possessed with patience greater than that of the enemy; thus, the desist strategy could not succeed either.

The JCS failed to secure the adoption of the win strategy along with the means and conditions to accomplish it because of its weakened influence. The legal strengthening of the Office of the Secretary of Defense and the dominating intellect and personality of Robert S. McNamara were major factors in the decline of the JCS. Moreover, Lyndon B. Johnson's general suspicion of the military kept the military on the defensive. In addition, the eroding professional ethics of the military destroyed the integrity of the reporting system, resulting in optimistic reports and claims of capabilities that were much higher than reality. Finally, the win strategy failed because, although the United States knew what Sino-Soviet military capabilities were, President Johnson and his advisers, to include the military, could never be certain of Sino-Soviet intentions.

Thus, the fear of Sino-Soviet military capabilities worldwide dictated that gradual application of military power even though so doing violated almost all of the military principles of war.

The gradual application of military power cannot bring a quick victory if, indeed, it can bring victory at all. Apart from its gradual application, United States military power was not, for the most part, effectively applied against the rear bases of the enemy. Ironically, the United States applied most of its combat power inside the borders of its ally South Vietnam.

It would be simplistic to blame the failure of the United States effort in Southeast Asia upon one segment or another of American society. It was not the president or the Congress or the press or the military or the members of the anti-war movements alone that caused our failure. The mistakes of Vietnam cannot be laid at the feet of any one person or group. They were more systemic than personal—the result of dynamics impelled by the Cold War moving in a stream of complete or partial successes until they went one war too far.

Until Vietnam, we had no real sense that our power was finite. There was, perhaps, no way to know we had gone too far until we had gone too far. Perhaps, the United States had to make this mistake once. We had to learn an important lesson: American political and military power has certain limits and must not be overextended into areas in which Sino-Soviet military capabilities dictate the adoption of unsound military strategies. In areas absolutely vital to the survival and success of liberty, the United States must be prepared to employ, if necessary, the *full* range of its military capabilities within the framework of sound grand and military strategy.

But in our rush to ensure that our future use of power is neither arrogant or undisciplined or unwise, we may have lost sight of the essentiality of having power. The cure for the mistakes of the past is not unilateral disarmament. Despite the efforts of President Obama, enfeebling ourselves militarily is not a useful exercise in humility or discipline. The United States used its military power poorly, and perhaps unnecessarily, in Vietnam. The consequences have been serious. But the abandonment of military power would have been fatal.

Thus, we have come full circle and back to statesmanship's most exacting task: making wise decisions. But the statesman does not have to bear his burden alone. There are, or should be, those who can provide sound advice. The quality of the decisions made by the American commander-in-chief rests, in large measure, upon the quality of the advice received from military advisers. The degree to which the president listens to them depends upon the quality of the men and women in the military. Crucial to our continued existence in a dangerous world is the development of quality military advisers and mutual understanding between the civil representatives of the State and the leaders of the armed forces.

Formula for Failure in Vietnam

The civil-military relationship is essentially a feudal contract, the civil authority is the master, and the military is the servant. Despite the dominance of the civilian leadership, each has certain responsibilities toward the other, and as in any contract, both parties must perform according to its terms.

The civilian government's first obligation is to define clearly its vital interests and to evolve a comprehensive policy or grand strategy to achieve or defend them.

Because modern society is so complicated, the civilian leadership cannot accomplish its primary task without input from sub-groups in the society possessed of specialized knowledge. In this case, the military must examine the vital interests and the policy aims of the government to determine the monetary and human costs necessary to accomplish successfully the aims of policy. This is simply, "the coordination of national policy with the power to enforce it."

This coordination, however, rests upon the assumption that the advice from the professional military will be honest—that its ethnological foundations will be cast in the cement of duty, honor, and service to country and that, above all else, the assessments of the military will come cleansed of institutional self-interest and personal advancement. Therefore, if the military is to play its rightful role in the civil-military relationship in the twenty-first century, its first task must be to get its own house in order.

But the United States Army may not be able to recapture its professional ethos by evolutionary methods. It will be decades before it is rid of those officers who ticket-punched their way to high rank by embracing the sociological experiments forced upon it during the Obama Administration. Furthermore, it is natural that those who rose by such means will select their own replacements from the ranks of those who were their junior accomplices. Some mirrors are hard to break.

Thus, the Army may be too large an organization to identify and purge all those who succumbed to the institutional pressures to produce good news and to look good at all times. What is needed now is for the Army to demonstrate that honest reporting will be rewarded rather than punished.

The quickest way to do that would be to alter radically the instructions given to promotion boards. Instead of instructing them to select for promotion only those officers with perfect mirror-image records of their own, they should also look for some iconoclasts and some who have gone down swinging over issues of principle. In due course, the officer corps would get the message that standing up for what is right is not a one-way ticket to the dustbin. This would result in some modest improvement, but it will not be a cure-all because the Army's evaluation system for its officers is hopelessly flawed by its subjectivity. Until the observations of peers and, especially, subordinates are brought into the evaluation process in a meaningful way, the Army will continue to have to rely upon the subjective opinions of a rating and an endorsing officer. Fooling these two officials is done routinely. Fooling one's peers is difficult. Fooling one's subordinates is almost impossible.

Competition can be very useful in motivating individuals and units to greater effort, but it can get out of hand. When that happens and it is tied to promotion, the test results are upgraded by some mysterious process. In time, training suffers because it is simpler to omit the training and merely forward the scores. The Army must guard against this and ruthlessly purge those who cannot resist the temptation to do this, but the Army must also reduce the pressures that make this temptation so great. In 1965, Captain Peter M. Dawkins recognized this danger by saying that the Army needed to give its officers and NCOs the "Freedom to Fail," in peacetime. Hopefully, this point will be understood someday.

The quality of military advice is a function of the preparation of the officer corps producing the service chiefs. Congress must continue to interest itself in the school systems of the armed services to ensure the subjects engaged are meaningful but, more importantly, that the professional ethos transmitted and inculcated is in accord with the traditions of the services as the repository of the highest human values. Punishing military instructors for teaching from the standard texts about Islam or about any political ideology based on some super-sensitive application of political correctness eats at the heart of academic freedom.

The Wehrmacht generals told Hitler that Germany could not pursue successfully an aggressive foreign policy leading to the destabilization of the balance of power in Europe. Hitler confounded his generals by his early successes, but they were due more to the weakness of the Allies and their foreign policy failures than they were due to any genius of Hitler. In the end, the older generals were correct, but most of them were not around when the Third Reich was destroyed. Hitler, backed by a Nazi *Reichstag,* could do anything he wanted in foreign and military affairs. The lesson for Americans should be obvious.

Flowing from the proper coordination of national policy and the military capability to enforce it is grand strategy. Because little in the background of the average commander-in-chief prepares him to become the nation's grand strategist, he needs the advice of military professionals—not to dominate the grand strategy formulation process but to provide, in clear-cut terms, the military components of the grand strategy equation.

In order to give proper credence to the offerings of the military, the president must be satisfied that the military leadership does indeed know what it is talking about and has not been misled by optimistic reports stemming from promotion-centered dishonesty or by institutional self-aggrandizement. Then and only then, can the other mechanics of the civil-military contract come into operation. With the grand strategy based upon the best possible military advice (and hopefully sound advice from the other elements of the government) the military strategies needed to accomplish the grand strategy can be evolved.

It is at this point, however, that the military must be protected against dilettantism by non-military "experts." This is not to say the military should be allowed to develop military strategy in a vacuum. Indeed, the military should be provided and take advantage of the best advice it can get—but in the same manner that the military only *advises* the commander-in-chief on grand strategy formulation, they should not have *military* strategy dictated to it by outsiders. But, in order for the aims of policy to be accomplished successfully, the commander-in-chief must carefully supervise the military to insure the strategies they develop actually address the aims of policy. Thus, throughout this give-and-take process there must be the element of civilian control of the military without interfering with the development of the essentially military portions of military strategy formulation.

Once the military strategy has been determined to be appropriate to achieve the aims of policy, then the civilian society must provide the military with adequate means to do so and then ensure that the strategy is undertaken under favorable conditions.

Tactics—the art of executing plans and handling forces in battle—is the province of the military; however, the civilian leadership must make certain the war as a whole is conducted in accordance with whatever laws of warfare the society accepts.

But what if the military feels that the only military strategy that the civilian leadership will approve is unworkable? What if the military strategy is sound enough but inadequate means are provided for its accomplishment or it is not allowed to be undertaken under favorable conditions? What then is the duty of the military under its contract?

VIII. One War Too Far

It is suggested here that even though theirs is an autocratic or feudal contract, the civilian master did not intend to contract with his military servant for a military defeat. Indeed, the purpose of the contract is to achieve the aims of policy. It is not to achieve the destruction of the master and his servant. This imputes to the servant the need to say to his master, "If I try to do your bidding without adequate means and/or under unfavorable conditions it will result in our mutual destruction. Master, I am certain that was not your intention. I cannot, as your loyal servant, execute the military strategy you have approved under these circumstances. For this reason, you must find someone else to carry out your orders, because I cannot, as your loyal servant, be the instrument of your destruction."

Why, one might ask, did not the American military during the Vietnam War make such a presentation to the civilian leadership? Perhaps—we can never say—it should be kept in mind the Vietnam situation did not meet exactly the situation in the above scenario. The loss of the Vietnam War may have been a diplomatic and military disaster, but it did not destroy the United States. Clearly, the war cost the United States dearly in lives, in treasure, in a divided society, in a lost sense of national purpose and, perhaps, a permanently damaged national will. Even so, our adversaries would be foolish to push the United States too far—particularly in Central America and along our southern border.

We have endured the shock of the highly visible debacle as in Saigon as Americans and South Vietnamese scrabbled aboard those final departing helicopters, departing from the CIA station chief's rooftop. Not from the U.S. Embassy, as so often misreported. We endured 444 days of national paralysis while revolutionary Iran held 53 Americans hostage. And, during that time, we saw the charred remains of American aircraft smoldering in the Iranian desert the evidence of the failure of a commando-style raid launched in hope of rescuing the American hostages. We sat numbed as our Marines picked through the rubble of a poorly secured compound in Beirut looking for the remains of their comrades. And, later, we saw our new embassy in Beirut destroyed, as well. And, most telling of all, radical Islamists destroyed the World Trade Center, damaged the Pentagon and, were it not for the bravery of the passengers aboard United Airlines Flight 93, our Capitol or the White House might have been destroyed as well.

Apparently, we have either failed to learn the lessons of Vietnam or learned the wrong lessons. The Reagan Administration put an end to President Carter's tilt toward national disarmament. Then, after the Clinton Administration spent the so-called "peace dividend" on social welfare programs, President George W. Bush rebuilt our military once again, only to see President Obama virtually destroy it. Such steep ascents and downward spirals waste men, machines and send uncertain signals to those who would harm us.

Rebuilding our military strength is a badly needed first step, but there is little evidence that we have learned very much about when, where and how to use military force. For example, the U.S. still has troops deployed in Afghanistan—that "graveyard of empires."

The true lesson of Vietnam should tell us—but only when our vital national interests are at stake—to give unstinting economic and political support to those who seek the realization of stable, representative governments based on the principles contained in our own Declaration of Independence. But, if we are to survive the assaults by radical Islam from without and from within and if are to survive the storm of illegal immigrants that is gathering in Central and South America, those who fashion our grand strategy must put America first and foremost in their thinking. And they must be willing to listen to professional military advice when military responses are appropriate to our survival as a nation.

Sound military advice should include an insistence on denying sanctuaries to the enemy, and on having the means and the latitude to accomplish the aims of grand strategy. Those are lessons we never seem to learn.

Epilogue

For all sad words of tongue and pen, the saddest are these,
"It might have been."
　　　　　　　—John Greenleaf Whittier (1807–1892)

In order to win the presidential election of 1968, President Richard M. Nixon promised to find a "peace with honor" solution to the Vietnam War. As his negotiating partner, he chose Dr. Heinz Alfred "Henry" Kissinger; first, in 1969, as his national security adviser and, in 1973, as his secretary of state.

To get the North Vietnamese to the bargaining table in Paris, the U.S. used its formidable air armada based on aircraft carriers in the South China Sea, on the B-52 bombers based on Guam, and on fighter-bombers based in Thailand and in South Vietnam. The first attempt was called Linebacker I. Armed with mostly tactical fighter-bombers, Linebacker I was designed to drive North Vietnamese incursions into South Vietnam back into North Vietnam and to get the North Vietnamese to the bargaining table. When Linebacker I did not get the North Vietnamese to the bargaining table, the next effort was called Linebacker II, consisting mainly of B-52 bombers that did what the Joint Chiefs of Staff had been advocating all along: Bomb and mine the North Vietnamese harbors and bomb Hanoi, the capital city of North Vietnam. Linebacker II was also known as the "Christmas Bombing."

The combined results of Linebacker I and II were the release of the American POWS and the eventual arrival of a North Vietnamese delegation in Paris. Suddenly, the North Vietnamese Politburo realized that the Nixon-Kissinger team was far different from that of President Lyndon B. Johnson and his whiz kid micro-managers left over from the Kennedy Administration. Moreover, the NVA, and especially the Viet Cong, had suffered a serious defeat during Tet 1968 which further increased the desire of the North Vietnamese leadership to get the United States out of South Vietnam.

Epilogue

Regarding Vietnam, Dr. Kissinger's long career is, arguably, most notable for teaming with North Vietnam's Le Duc Tho to negotiate the Paris Peace Accords of 1973. Consequently, both men were awarded the Noble Peace Prize.

Le Duc Tho, however, rejected the prize outright, saying peace was not at hand. He was correct in that the North Vietnamese Army had no intention of observing the ceasefire called for by the Paris Accords. The NVA continued its practice of seizing border areas south of the 17th parallel and along the Laotian and Cambodia borders with South Vietnam. The South Vietnamese Army would attempt to recover the lost ground, with mixed results. Thus, between 1973 and 1975, the ceasefire was more honored in the breach than in fact. The breaches, although relatively minor, were so many that the multi-national, International Control and Supervision Commission (ICCS), created by the Paris Accords to police the cease fire, proved ineffective and withdrew in despair.

Dr. Kissinger accepted the peace prize; however, he donated his prize money to a fund for the children of American service members either killed or wounded in the war. Later, after the fall of Saigon in 1975, Dr. Kissinger attempted to return his Nobel Peace Prize.

From the American point of view, the Paris Accords were somewhat satisfactory in that the North Vietnamese promised to recognize the existing government of South Vietnam as legitimate and they would not use its regular forces to invade South Vietnam. But the North Vietnamese refused to recognize the 17th Parallel as the official border between North and South Vietnam, the line at which the Nixon Administration hoped to restore the *status quo ante bellum*. Even so, it is highly doubtful that the North Vietnamese would have complied with such a provision. And, more significantly, while the North Vietnamese were required to withdraw their armed forces from their sanctuaries in Laos and Cambodia, they did not do so.

Bear in mind that South Vietnam's entire western border, from Laos in the north on south to the southern tip of Cambodia, was already infiltrated with North Vietnamese troops, enjoying sanctuary in both Laos and Cambodia. With South Vietnam's entire western border exposed to the NVA, it would be a simple matter for the NVA to thrust eastward along Provincial Route QL 19 and Provincial Route QL 21, effectively slicing South Vietnam into three segments. Such thrusts would, perforce, draw the South Vietnamese Army south from its most northern provinces along the DMZ to defend against the twin columns being directed at the geographic middle of South Vietnam and toward the South Vietnamese capital of Saigon.

Once the South Vietnamese Army withdrew southward along the coastal plain connecting Hue and Da Nang, the armored, tracked, and wheeled vehicles of the North Vietnam Army would have easy going down the famed *La Rue Sans Joie* (National Route QL 1), all the way down the coast from the DMZ to Saigon.

In order to win the grudging agreement of South Vietnamese President Nguyen Van Thieu for the Paris Peace Accords, the United States made a solemn pledge to resupply South Vietnam with arms and ammunition for its defense and, in the case of an invasion by North Vietnam, to bring American force of arms, presumably air power, to the aid of the South Vietnamese.

As a result of the Paris Accords, all U.S. combat troops were withdrawn from South Vietnam. U.S. combat operations versus North Vietnam were halted. After 1973, all that remained of the American presence on the ground in South Vietnam were some teams of logistics personnel charged with the turnover to the South Vietnamese armed forces of the supplies and equipment the U.S. wanted them to have and/ or were simply too uneconomical to ship stateside.

But that was not the end of American air power in Southeast Asia. Standing just off the east coast of South Vietnam in the South China Sea were three U.S. Navy carrier strike forces. Each with a complement of about 72 fighter-bombers. On the nearby island of Guam, an entire B-52 wing was still at the ready. Moreover, the U.S. Forces retained a very robust fighter-bomber presence at air bases in nearby Thailand.

Thus, if so ordered, the United States had enough combat air power available to crater *La Rue Sans Joie* all the way from the DMZ to Saigon. Plus, the U.S. retained enough air power to interdict QL 19 that runs across South Vietnam from Du Co on the Cambodian border to the port of Qui Nhon. The less improved OL 21 from Ban Me Thuot in Dak Lak Province to the port of Nha Trang would have been even easier to interdict.

Status Quo Ante Bellum

Throughout the Kennedy, Johnson, Nixon, and Ford Administrations, the U.S. Congress was under the control of the Democratic Party which, due to the mishandling of the Vietnam War by President Johnson, had turned on the Democrat Johnson and was even less in a mood to be helpful to the Republicans, Richard Nixon and Gerald Ford.

After the withdrawal of American ground forces in 1973, South Vietnam, with the exception of the relatively low-level back and forth battles along the DMZ at the 17th parallel and along the Laotian and Cambodian borders, enjoyed a relatively peaceful existence. The South Vietnamese armed forces seemed to have matters adequately in hand and some people were even talking about "peace for our time."

But then, in March 1975, the NVA launched a major attack out of its Cambodian sanctuary aimed at the capture of Ban Me Thuot, the capital of Dak Lak Province. But, instead of pressing that attack all the way forward, the NVA paused to see if the United States would fulfill it pledges under the Paris Accords, or not. When the United States failed to respond in any meaningful way, the Politburo in Hanoi decided the United States had washed its hands of South Vietnam and ordered all-out assaults designed to take the NVA all the way across South Vietnam to the South China Sea and down National Route QL 1 all the way to Saigon.

By May 3, 1975, the NVA controlled all of Vietnam. How could this happen? There are six reasons, some of them subject to debate:

First, the Democrat-controlled Congress passed legislation on July 1, 1973, cutting off additional military aid to South Vietnam. And, on November 7, 1973, Congress overrode President Nixon's veto of that legislation.

Secondly, because of the crippling effect of Watergate and the installation of the mandate-less Gerald Ford as President of the United States, the North Vietnamese Politburo perceived the United States as a toothless tiger.

Thirdly, the Paris Accord was flawed from the outset because the agreement permitted the NVA to maintain its existing forces inside the territory of South Vietnam.

Fourth, the impact of "Vietnamization" was to train and equip the South Vietnamese Army to be heavily dependent on U.S. technology, skilled technological support, and spare parts. The U.S. withdrawal of its technical expertise was too precipitous to teach the South Vietnamese what they needed to know about operating a technical armed force.

Fifth, the refusal of the U.S. to respond to the repeated violations of the Paris Accords' ceasefire by the North Vietnamese caused the North Vietnamese to believe that they had been given a free hand in Southeast Asia.

Finally, it should be noted *both* the North Vietnamese and the United States failed to abide by the pledges they made in the Paris Accords. The

North Vietnamese violated the Paris Accords by its invasion of South Vietnam in March 1975. The United States violated the Paris Accords and its agreements with South Vietnam by failing to come to the aid of South Vietnam.

In the end, the Paris Accords, no matter how well-intended, left the South Vietnamese, due to the NVA's sanctuaries in Laos and Cambodia, in a strategically and tactically impossible situation. A situation that depended upon the North Vietnamese keeping their pledges. Or, in case of all-out attack by the NVA, a situation that could only be rectified by the massive application of American airpower.

Could the reapplication of American airpower have saved South Vietnam from falling behind the Bamboo Curtain? That, of course, is one of history's imponderables. But we do know the chance to at least achieve the *status quo ante bellum* was lost forever.

"When Will They Ever Learn?"

But what of today in Afghanistan and in Iraq? Is the United States guilty of making the same sanctuary mistakes it made in Vietnam?

In the wake of the attacks of September 11, 2001, a combination of U.S. Special Forces, horse-mounted clandestine agents of the CIA, and the Afghan's Northern Alliance routed al-Qaeda from its training bases in Afghanistan. Unfortunately, Osama bin Laden, Mullah Omar and many of their followers were able to escape into the sanctuary of Pakistan.

Rightly or wrongly, the United States then attempted to move the peoples of Afghanistan in the direction of a Jeffersonian Democracy. Unfortunately, the warlords who have always run the graveyard of empires were not interested in Jeffersonian Democracy nor were they about to give up the powers they held for centuries under a variety of invaders be they Russian, Great Britain, China or even as far back as Alexander the Great. Consequently, Afghanistan ranks as the longest war in which the United States has engaged its armed forces.

In the case of Afghanistan, not only are demographics fate (the tribal warlord system), but geography as well. Afghanistan is a landlocked country bordered by six nations and one disputed territory: Turkmenistan, Uzbekistan, Tajikistan, China, Iran, and, of course, Pakistan. Any and all of those countries are available to provide sanctuary to the forces of al-Qaeda and to the Taliban.

Epilogue

Assuming it would have been possible to convert Afghanistan from its feudal-warlord system to even a semblance of a Jeffersonian Democracy, how would that have addressed the vital interests of the United States? And why should such an attempt be made, given that Afghanistan's geographic position surrounds it with sanctuaries?

When the tests called for in *Sound Military Decision* are applied to Afghanistan, the graveyard of empires fails every test. The aim did not address a long-term vital interest of the United States. The objective was unclear. The aim was not attainable. The means allotted were inadequate. And the conditions were immensely unfavorable.

The situation in Iraq, however, was not quite as formidable. While Iraq is not landlocked, enjoying a meager 36-mile waterfront on the Persian Gulf, Iraq is surrounded by Jordan, Syria, Turkey, Iran, Kuwait, and Saudi Arabia. Once again, potential sanctuaries abound in almost every direction.

With perfect hindsight, it can be said the U.S.–led invasion of Iraq in March of 2003 was a classic case of inadequate intelligence and a failure to look ahead to the geopolitical consequences of a military victory.

Once again, as they did in Afghanistan, our armed forces, brilliantly led by General Tommy Franks, produced a quick and decisive military victory. The aim was to find and destroy Saddam Hussein's ability to wage nuclear/chemical warfare on his neighbors. But the Israeli attack on the Iran's Osirak reactor in 1981 had already caused Saddam to shutter his nuclear weapons program, although Saddam continued to boast that his nuclear weapons program still existed. A boast that ended with Saddam Hussein dangling at the end of a rope.

But the larger problem with the invasion of Iraq was that it removed Iraq as a geographic impediment to the western expansion of the influence of Iran in the Middle East. Saddam Hussein's brutal regime was supported by the world's fourth largest army. While the aim of making sure Saddam Hussein did not possess nuclear weapons was sound. Disbanding the world's fourth largest army that was blocking Iran's drive to achieve hegemony over the entire Middle East was a major geopolitical mistake.

Granted, Iran would still be able to spend millions of its oil and gas revenues to support terrorist organizations throughout the Middle East, but Iran would not have been in the position it was to lure the Obama Administration into an agreement (that was never ratified by the U.S. Senate) that put Iran on an eventual glide path to becoming a nuclear power and an even more existential threat to the State of Israel and to the entire region.

Epilogue

One of the major mistakes made by the administration of President George W. Bush was to place the management of post-invasion Iraq into the hands of the U.S. Department of State. What was needed in Iraq was a strong ruler along the lines of General Douglas MacArthur in postwar Japan. Moreover, instead of being entirely dismissed, the Sunni rank and file of Saddam's armed forces should have been retained in place to maintain order. While Saddam's top Sunni generals deserved to be dismissed, the other ranks could have played a useful role in maintaining order. Instead, the dismissed leadership of Saddam's armed forces (some of them quite capable) became the core of an insurgency simply because they no longer had jobs or anything else to do.

Consequently, the Bush Administration made enemies of the Sunni forces needed to maintain order across Iraq. With its former Sunni minders out of the way, the path was open for Iraq's Shiite majority to oppose the coalition occupation and to open the path for Shiite insurgents to flood into eastern Iraq from Shiite Iran.

It took the Bush Administration a long time to realize that winning a highly mechanized desert war against Saddam's conventional forces was far different from trying to prevail over a guerrilla insurgency being controlled from neighboring Iran. After some recalibration of tactics, along with a surge of an additional 20,000 troops, by 2010, the United States achieved a semblance of the 2003 *status quo ante*. Moreover, the brutality of Saddam and his sons was no more.

But a new president, who took office in 2009, placed constraining Rules of Engagement (ROE) on military operations in Iraq and then withdrew all U.S. forces from Iraq in December 2012, giving new energy to the Shiite insurgents pummeling Iraq from the East, and giving rise to the creation of ISIS, a nascent radical Islamist state in northern Iraq and Syria.

Which was the larger geopolitical mistake? The 2003 invasion of Iraq or the precipitous withdraw of U.S. forces in 2012? History will have to be the judge of that.

While many know that the United States lost more than 58,000 brave men and women in Vietnam and over 300,000 were wounded, it should be noted that 39,996 of those who died were just 22 or younger. Indeed, 8,283 of them were just 19. Virtually all of them were draftees who answered a call to duty orchestrated by their civilian masters in Washington, D.C.

While the administrations of both President George H.W. Bush and President George W. Bush were willing to allow our military the freedom

Epilogue

of action that was missing in the Vietnam War and allowed adequate means to support the war aims of the U.S.–led coalitions, the problem was, once again, that the aims did not square with the vital interests of the United Sates and that the existence of the sanctuaries around Afghanistan and Iraq made the aims impossible to attain.

There is a refrain from a pacifist folk song from the mid–1950s. You didn't need be a pacifist to embrace the question it posed—indeed, the most gung-ho, pro-war militarists may have demanded an answer. The song was Pete Seeger's "Where Have All the Flowers Gone?" The refrain was: "When will they ever learn? When will they ever learn?"

Glossary

ARVN: Army of the Republic of Vietnam

CIA: Central Intelligence Agency

CIDG: Civilian Irregular Defense Group. Indigenous tribesmen of the South Vietnamese border regions recruited to assist the U.S. Army Special Forces

CJCS: Chairman, Joint Chiefs of Staff

COMUSMACV: Commander, U.S. Military Assistance Command, Vietnam

CINCLANT: Commander-in-Chief, Atlantic

CINCPAC: Commander-in-Chief, Pacific

CORDS: Civil Operations and Development Support. Agency in Vietnam that directed overall pacification effort after 1967

CG: Counter-guerrilla

CUSA: Chief of Staff, U.S. Army

DMZ: Demilitarized Zone

DOD: Department of Defense

DRV: Democratic Republic of Vietnam (North Vietnam)

EUCOM: United States European Command

HES: Hamlet Evaluation System

ISA: International Security Affairs (a major agency of DOD)

JCS: Joint Chiefs of Staff

JUSPAO: Joint U.S. Public Affairs Office (for U.S. activities in South Vietnam)

MACV: Military Assistance Command, Vietnam

NVN: North Vietnam

NVA: North Vietnamese Army

NATO: North Atlantic Treaty Organization

NSAM: National Security Action Memorandum

Glossary

ORSA: Operations Research/Systems Analysis

OSD: Office of the Secretary of Defense

PF: Popular Forces (South Vietnamese paramilitary forces organized for local hamlet defense)

RF: Regional Forces (South Vietnamese home guards organized to defend local areas)

RVNAF: Republic of Vietnam, Armed Forces

ROK: Republic of Korea (South Korea)

SACEUR: Supreme Allied Commander, Europe

SANCTUARY: A safe haven from U.S. attack

Sappers: North Vietnamese soldiers trained to undermine and destroy fire base perimeter defenses and other installations

SEATO: Southeast Asia Treaty Organization

SECDEF: Secretary of Defense

SVN: South Vietnam

TAOR: Tactical Area of Responsibility

USARV: U.S. Army, Vietnam

USAID: U.S. Agency for International Development

USIA: U.S. Information Agency

UW: Unconventional Warfare

VC: Viet Cong

Bibliography

Primary Sources

Memoirs and Major Works by Civilian and Military Officials

Acheson, Dean. *Present at the Creation.* New York: W.W. Norton & Co., 1969.

Ball, George W. *The Discipline of Power.* New York: Little, Brown & Co., 1968.

Bradford, Zeb B., Jr., Lt. Colonel, USA, and Frederic J. Brown, Lt. Colonel, USA. *The United States Army in Transition.* Beverly Hills: Sage Nations, 1973.

Broughton, Jacksel M., Colonel, USA. *Thud Ridge.* Philadelphia: J.B. Lippincott, 1969.

Bunting, Josiah, Major, USA. *The Lionheads.* New York: George Braziller, 1972.

Burruss, L. H. "Bucky," Lt. Colonel, USA (Ret.) *Mike Force.* iUniverse, 2001.

_____. *Clash of Steel.* iUniverse, 2001.

_____. *A Mission for Delta.* iUniverse, 2001.

Clarke, Bruce C., General, USA (Ret.). *Guidelines for the Leader and Commander.* Harrisburg, PA: Stackpole Books, 1963.

Collins, Arthur S., Jr., Lt. General, USA (Ret.). *Common Sense Training: A Primer for Commanders.* San Rafael, CA: Presidio Press, 1978.

Dulles, Allen. *The Craft of Intelligence.* New York: Harper & Row, 1963.

Eccles, Henry E., Rear Admiral, USN (Ret.). *Military Concepts and Philosophy.* New Brunswick, NJ: Rutgers University Press, 1965.

Enthoven, Alain, and Wayne K. Smith. *How Much Is Enough?* New York: Harper & Row, 1971.

Franks, Tommy, General, USA (Ret.) *American Soldier.* New York: HarperCollins, 2004.

Gerhardt, Igor D. "Duke" Gerhardt. *The Eye of the Tiger.* Self-published, 2009.

Giap, Vo Nguyen, General. *Big Victory, Great Task.* New York: Westport, CT: Praeger, 1966.

_____. *People's War, People's Army.* Hanoi. Foreign Languages Publishing House, 1969.

Goodpaster, Andrew J., General, USA (Ret.). *For the Common Defense.* D.C. Heath, 1977.

Gravel, Mike, U.S. Senator (ed.). *The Senator Gravel Edition: The Pentagon Papers.* Boston: Beacon Press, 1971, Vol. IV.

Hamilton-Merritt, Jane. *Tragic Mountains: The Hmong, the Americans, and the Secret Wars for Laos, 1942–1992.* Bloomington: Indiana University Press, 1993.

Hartke, Vance, U.S. Senator. *The American Crisis in Vietnam.* Indianapolis: Bobbs-Merrill, 1968.

Hauser, William L., Lt. Colonel, USA. *America's Army in Crisis.* Baltimore: The Johns Hopkins University Press, 1973.

Herbert, Anthony B. *Soldier.* New York: Holt, Rinehart & Winston, 1973.

Bibliography

Hilsman, Roger. *The Politics of Policy Making in Defense and Foreign Affairs.* New York: Harper & Row, 1971.

_____. *To Move a Nation.* New York: Doubleday & Co., 1967.

Hoang Van Chi. *From Colonialism to Communism.* New York: Westport, CT: Praeger, 1964.

Hoopes, Townsend. *The Limits of Intervention.* Philadelphia: David McKay Co., 1969.

Johnson, Lyndon B. *The Vantage Point.* New York: Holt, Rinehart & Winston, 1971.

Kennan, George F. *American Diplomacy, 1900–1950.* New York: Mentor Books, 1951.

Kennedy, John F. *The Strategy of Peace.* New York: New York: Harper & Brothers, 1960.

Kennedy, Robert F. *Thirteen Days.* New York: W.W. Norton & Co., 1969.

Kinnard, Douglas, Brigadier General, USA (Ret.). *The War Managers.* Hanover, NH: Press of New England, 1977.

Kirkpatrick, Lyman B., Jr. *The Real CIA.* New York: Macmillan, 1969.

LeMay, Curtis E., General, USAF (Ret.). *America Is in Danger.* New York: Harper & Row, 1968.

Lodge, Henry Cabot. *The Storm Has Many Eyes.* New York: W.W. Norton & Co., Inc., 1973.

Mann, Scott. *Game Changers: Going Local to Defeat Violent Extremists.* Tribal Analysis Center of Leesburg, VA, 2017.

McGowan, Joe, Jr. *From Fidel Castro to Mother Teresa.* Broomfield, CO: Lac Amora Publishing, 2012.

McNamara, Robert S. *The Essence of Security.* New York: Harper & Row, 1968.

Moore, Harold G., and Joseph L. Galloway. *We Are Soldiers Still: A Journey Back to the Battlefields of Vietnam.* New York: Harper Perennial, 2009.

_____. *We Were Soldiers Once ... and Young.* New York: Random House, 1992.

Palmer, David, Colonel, USA. *Summons of the Trumpet.* San Rafael, CA: Presidio Press, 1977.

Palmer, John McAuley, Brigadier General, USA (Ret.). *America in Arms.* Yale University Press, 1941.

Peers, William R., Lt. General, USA (Ret.). *The Agony of My Lai.* W.W. Norton, 1978.

Piotrowski, "Pete," General, USAF (Ret.). *From Basic Airman to General: The Secret War and Other Conflicts.* New York: Exlibris Press, 2014.

Powell, Colin L. General, USA (Ret.). *My American Journey.* Random House, 1995.

Ridgway, Matthew B., General, USA (Ret.). *The Korean War.* New York: Doubleday & Co., 1967.

_____. *Soldier.* New York: Harper & Brothers, 1956.

Rostow, W. W. *The Diffusion of Power.* New York: Macmillan, 1972.

Schandler, Herbert Y., Lt. Colonel, USA (Ret.). *The Unmaking of a President.* Princeton, NJ: Princeton University Press, 1977.

Schlesinger, Arthur. *A Thousand Days.* Boston: Houghton Mifflin, 1965.

Singlaub, John K. Major General, USA (Ret.). *Hazardous Duty.* New York: Summit Books, 1991.

Sorensen, Theodore C. *Kennedy.* New York: Harper & Row, 1965.

Taylor, Maxwell D., General, USA (Ret.). *Precarious Security.* New York: W.W. Norton & Co., Inc., 1976.

_____. *Responsibility and Response.* New York: Harper & Row, 1967.

_____. *Swords and Plowshares.* New York: W.W. Norton & Co., Inc., 1972.

_____. *The Uncertain Trumpet.* New York: Harper & Brothers, 1959.

Thompson, Sir Robert. *No Exit from Vietnam.* London: Chatto & Windus, 1969.

Bibliography

_____. *Peace Is Not at Hand.* Philadelphia: David McKay Co., 1974.

Twinning, Nathan F., General, USAF (Ret.). *Neither Liberty nor Safety.* New York: Holt, Rinehart & Winston, 1960.

Upton, Emory, Brigadier General, USA. *The Armies of Asia and Europe.* London: Forgotten Books, 2018.

_____. *The Military Policy of the United States.* Washington, D.C.: United States Government Printing Office, 1917.

Walt, Lewis W., General, USMC (Ret.). *Strange War, Strange Strategy.* New York: Funk & Wagnalls, 1970.

Walton, George, Colonel, USA (Ret.). *The Tarnished Blade.* New York: New York: Dodd, Mead & Co., 1973.

Westmoreland, William C., General, USA (Ret.). *A Soldier Reports.* New York: Doubleday & Co., 1976.

Wisely, H. Denny, Rear Admiral, USN (Ret.). *Green Ink: Memoirs of a Fighter Pilot.* Self-Published, 2018.

Yost, Charles. *The Conduct and Misconduct of Foreign Affairs.* New York: Random House, 1972.

_____. *The Insecurity of Nations.* Westport, CT: Praeger, 1969.

Personal Interviews

Anderson, George, Admiral, USN (Ret.). Former Chief of Naval Operations. Division and Field Force Commander. March 1971, Washington, D.C.

Berry, Robert W. Former General Counsel of the Army and Member of the OSA General Counsel Staff. 13–14, December 1977, Washington, D.C.

Bhaskar, Surindar N., Major General, USA. Assistant Surgeon General, U.S. Army. 10 October 1977, Miami Beach, FL.

Binder, Edward C., Major General. The Adjutant General, Nebraska National Guard. 13 March 1978, Lincoln, NE.

Cheatham, Joseph L., Brigadier General USA. Commander, U.S. Army Health Services Command. 11 October 1977, Miami Beach, FL.

Clarke, Bruce C., General, USA (Ret.). Former commander, U.S. Army, Europe. June 1971, Washington, D.C.

Collins, A. S., Jr., Lt. General, USA (Ret.). Former Deputy Commander, U.S, Army, Europe, and a Division and Field Commander in Vietnam. 14 December 1977, Alexandria, VA.

Cross, Leslie H., Colonel, USA (Ret.). Librarian, National Guard Assn. and Assistant Curator of National Guard Memorial Hall. 14 December 1977, Washington, D.C.

Decker, George, General, USA (Ret.). Former Chief of Staff, U.S. Army. March 1971, Washington, D.C.

Everson, Donald, Colonel, USAF. Former POW in "Hanoi Hilton." November 1976, Nellis Air Force Base, Nevada.

Forsythe, George I., Jr., Lt. General, USA. Special Assistant to the Chief of Staff for the Modern Volunteer Army. Summer 1971, The Pentagon.

Green, George O., Jr., Colonel, USA. Former Official in the U.S. Army Military Personnel Center. 15 February 1978, Lincoln, NE.

Hill, Thomas A. Assistant for Military and Civilian Affairs, National Guard Bureau. 13–14 December 1977, Washington, D.C.

Johnson, Harold K., General, USA (Ret.). Former Chief of Staff, U.S. Army. 13 December 1977, Washington, D.C.

Bibliography

Jordan, Amos A., Brigadier General, USA (Ret.). Former Member of ISA under John McNaughton and Former Chairman of Department of Social Science at the Military Academy. 13 December 1977, Washington, D.C.

Larsen, Stanley R., Lt. General, USA (Ret.). Former Commander, I U.S. Field Force, Vietnam. 8 November 1977, San Francisco, CA.

Lemnitzer, Lyman L., General, USA (Ret.). Former Chairman of the JCS and SACEUR. June 1971, 14 December 1977, Washington, D.C.

Lombard, Reginald T., Lt. Colonel, USA. Former Commander, 2nd Battalion, 5th Cavalry in Vietnam. 28 June 1977, Washington, D.C.

Mack, William P., Vice Admiral, USN (Ret.). Former Commander U.S. Seventh Fleet and Superintendent, U.S. Naval Academy. 11 December 1977, Alexandria, VA.

Milton, Theodore R., General, USAF (Ret.). Former Member of CINCPAC Staff and U.S. Representative to the NATO Military Council. 20 January 1978, Colorado Springs, CO.

Muggelberg, Glenn E., Brigadier General, USA (Ret.). Former Assistant Deputy Chief of Staff for Intelligence in Vietnam. 19 April 1977, Camp Roberts, CA.

Peers, William R., Lt. General, USA (Ret.). Former Division and Field Commander in Vietnam and Head of the Peers Commission Appointed to Investigate the My Lai Affair. 7 November 1977, Kentfield, CA.

Sparrow, Herbert G., Major General, USA (Ret.). Former Head of the Department of the Army Special Review Boards. 13 December 1977, Arlington, VA.

Waltman, Donald G., Colonel, USAF. Former POW in "Hanoi Hilton." 11 November 1976, Nellis Air Force Base, Nevada.

Telephone Interviews

Goodpaster, Andrew J., General, USA. Superintendent, United States Military Academy. 6 April 1978.

Karhohs, Fred E., Major General, USA (Ret.). Former Member of ISA and Assistant to Secretary McNamara. 12 February 1978.

Rusk, Dean. Secretary of State for Presidents Kennedy and Johnson. 5 January 1978.

Westmoreland, William C., General, USA (Ret.). Former Commander, U.S. Military Assistance Command, Vietnam and Chief of Staff, U.S. Army. 7 January 1978.

Letters to the Author Contributing Information, Assistance or Offers of Assistance

Atkeson, Edward B., Brigadier General, USA. 6 September 1977, 30 December 1977.

Berry, Robert W. January 10, 1978, 16 March 1978.

Bhaskar, Surindar N., Major General, USA. 12 September 1977.

Bissell, Richard M., Jr. 10 October 1977.

Blanchard, George S., General, USA. 9 November 1977, via his *aide-de-camp*, Major Frederick W. Timmerman, Jr.

Brady, Morris J., Major General, USA. 26 September 1977, 4 January 1978.

Clarke, Bruce C., General, USA (Ret.). 7 November 1977, 17 December 1977.

Davison, Michael S., General, USA (Ret.). 10 September 1977, 5 January 1978.

Decker, George H., General, USA (Ret.). 7 September 1977.

DePuy, William E., General, USA (Ret.). 8 September 1977, 27 December 1977.

Eggers, George D., Jr., Brigadier General, USA (Ret.). 15 September 1977, 29 January 1978.

Flanagan, Edward M., Jr., Lt. General, USA. 8 September 1977.

Bibliography

Forsythe, George I., Lt. General, USA (Ret.). 9 September 1977.

Freeman, Paul L., Jr., General, USA (Ret.). 15 September 1977, 18 December 1977.

Gard, Robert G., Jr., Lt. General, USA. 7 September 1977.

George, Arthur F., Colonel, USAF (Ret.). 31 July 1977.

Goodpaster, Andrew J., Lt. General, USA. 10 September 1977.

_____. Letter to General Bruce C. Clarke, USA (Ret.). 14 November 1977.

Gorman, Paul F., Major General, USA. 20 September 1977.

Haines, Ralph E., Jr., General, USA (Ret.). 11 September 1977.

Hamlett, Barksdale, General, USA (Ret.). 3 September 1977.

Harkins, Paul D., General, USA (Ret.). September 1977, 7 February 1978.

Hollingsworth, James F., Lt. General, USA (Ret.). 10 September 1977, 18 February 1978.

Howze, Hamilton H., General, USA (Ret.). 5 September 1977.

Johnson, Harold K., General, USA (Ret.). 27 September 1977.

Karhohs, Fred E., Major General, USA (Ret.). 6 September 1977, 16 January 1978.

Keeley, John B., Colonel, USA (Ret.). 14 March 1977, 7 April 1977, 18 May 1977, 24 June 1977, 11 July 1977, 2 August 1977, 18 August 1977, 1 September 1977, 3 November 1977, 9 January 1978, 12 January 1978, 23 January 1978, 4 February 1978, 7 February 1978, 6 March 1978, 10 March 1978.

Kingston, Joseph P., Major General, USA. 11 October 1977.

Kingston, Robert C., Major General, USA. September 1977, 11 January 1978.

Kirkpatrick, Lyman B. Professor at Brown University. September 1977, 14 February 1978. Included messages to the author from Professors David Hall and Harry Latimer.

Larsen, Stanley R., Lt. General, USA (Ret.). 5 September 1977, October 1977.

LeMay, Curtis E., General, USAF (Ret.). 6 September 1977.

Lemnitzer, Lyman L., General, USA (Ret.). 9 December 1977, 15 February 1978.

Livsey, William J., Major General, USA. 7 September 1977.

Lodge, Henry Cabot. Former United States Ambassador to RVN. 2 September 1977.

McChristian, Joseph A., Major General, USA (Ret.). 11 September 1977, 8 November 1977.

Menetrey, Louis C., Major General, USA. 5 September 1977, 30 December 1977.

Muggelberg, Glenn E., Brigadier General, USA (Ret.). 8 March 1977.

Nitze, Paul. Former Head of ISA, Deputy Secretary of Defense under Robert S. McNamara. 15 September 1977.

Norton, John, Lt. General, USA (Ret.). 7 September 1977.

Palmer, Bruce, Jr., General, USA (Ret.). 15 December 1977.

Pearson, Willard, Lt. General, USA (Ret.). 1 September 1977, 8 February 1978.

Peers, William R., Lt. General, USA (Ret.). 2 September 2, 1977, 1 November 1977.

Rattan, Donald V., Major General, USA (Ret.). 26 September 1977, 11 January 1978.

Rosson, William B., General, USA (Ret.). 2 October 1977, 11 January 1978.

Rostow, Eugene. Professor, Yale University and Former State Department Official in the Johnson Administration. 10 September 1977, 20 December 1977.

Rostow, Walter W. Professor, University of Texas and Former National Security Affairs Adviser to President Johnson. 2 September 1977, 28 December 1977.

St. John, Adrian II, Major General, USA (Ret.). 8 September 1977, 7 January 1978.

Seitz, Richard J., Lt. General, USA (Ret.). 5 September 1977.

Singlaub, John K., Major General, USA. 16 September 1977.

Smith, James C., Major General, USA. 13 September 13, 1977, 24 January 24, 1978.

Sparrow, Herbert G., Major General, USA (Ret.). 5 September 1977, 2 December 1977, 14 December 1977, 4 February 1978.

149

Bibliography

Starry, Donn A., General, USA. 9 September 1977, 4 January 1978.
Stilwell, Richard C., General, USA (Ret.). 15 October 1977.
Taylor, Maxwell D., General, USA (Ret.). 9 September 1977, 22 February 1978.
Timms, Charles J., Major General, USA (Ret.). 15 September 1977, 9 March 1978.
Tolson, John J., Lt. General, USA (Ret.). 15 September 1977, 14 January 1978.
Vinson, Wilbur H., Major General, USA. 21 September 1977, 28 December 1977.
Westmoreland, William C., General, USA (Ret.). 19 September 1977, 17 October 1977, 28 December 1977.
Yarborough, William P., Lt. General, USA (Ret.). 12 September 1977, 2 January 1978.
York, Robert H., Lt. General, USA (Ret.). 6 September 1977.
Zais, Melvin, General, USA (Ret.). 16 September 1977, 14 February 1978.
Zumwalt, Elmo, Admiral, USN (Ret.). 14 September 1977.

Articles by Civilian and Military Officials

Anderson, George W., Jr., Admiral, USN (Ret.). Speech before the National Press Club, September 4, 1963, *New York Times*, 5 September 1963, 19.
Bahnsen, John C., Colonel, USA, and R. William Highlander, Major, USA. "Writing a Readable OER," *Armor*, July–August 1976, 26–28.
"Boards Urged to Look Beyond OER," *Army Times*, 18 June 1975, 12.
Boatner, Mark M. III, Colonel, USA. "Seeing Ourselves as Others See Us ... First," *Army*, February 1971.
Breckinridge, W. M., Major General, USA (Ret.). "Why Army's Morale Declines," *Armed Forces Journal International*, July 1977, 6.
Brown, George S., General, USAF. "National Security Is Dependent Upon a Strong Defense," *Commanders Digest*, 17 November 1977, 2–3, 5–11.
Clifford, Clark M. "A Vietnam Reappraisal: The History of One Man's View of How It Evolved," *Foreign Affairs*, 47, July 1969, 601–622.
Dawkins, Peter M., Captain, USA. "Freedom to Fail," *Infantry*, September-October 1965, 8–10. General George Marshall Award Winner.
Dupuy, Trevor N., Colonel, USA (Ret.). "The Current Implications of German Military Excellence," *Strategic Review*, Fall 1976, 87–94.
Flanagan, Edward M., Jr., Lt. General, USA. "...and What's More, He's Always the Boss," *Army*, September 1977, 12.
Garvin, Richard F., Major, USA. "Troop Leaders Need Answers, Not Buzzwords," *Army*, April 1977, 24–25, 28–31.
Ginsburgh, Robert N., Brigadier General, USA. "The Challenge to Military Professionalism," *Foreign Affairs*, 42, October 1963–July 1964, 255–268.
Hamilton, William A., Captain, USA. "Adventure Training," *Army*, January 1966, 61–63.
Hamilton, William A., Lt. Colonel, USA. "The Decline and Fall of the Joint Chiefs of Staff," *US Naval War College Review*, April 1972, 36–58.
Hamilton, William A., Ph.D. "The Uncounted Enemy: A Media Deception," *CAUSA Magazine*, Winter 1986–87, 28–33.
Haponski, William, Lt. Colonel, USA. "Reply to a Vietnam Veteran," *Saturday Review*, 25 October 1969.
Hauser, William, L., Lt. Colonel, USA. "Professionalism and the Junior Officer Drain," *Army*, September 1970.
Higinbotham, Lewis, Lt. Colonel, USA. "Will to Win," *Infantry*, January–February 1976, 12–15.

Bibliography

Howze, Hamilton H., General, USA (Ret.). "Military Discipline and National Security," *Army*, January 1971.

_____. "Vietnam and the Aftermath of 'Peace,'" *Army*, July 1973, 5–7.

Kennan, George F. "The Sources of Soviet Conduct," *Foreign Affairs*, 25 July 1947, 566–582. (Author shown as X.)

Kennedy, William V., Colonel, USA. "It Takes More Than Talent to Cover a War," *Army*, July 1978, 23–26.

Kissinger, Henry A. "The Viet Nam Negotiations," *Foreign Affairs*, January 1969.

Lynn, William M., Major General, USA. "The Military Profession: What Is It?" *Army*, September 1971.

Mack, William P., Vice Admiral, USN (Ret.). "The Need for Dissent," *Army Times*, 12 January 1976, 20–24, 26.

Mataxis, Theodore C., Brigadier General, USA (Ret.). "On the Military's Right—and Duty—to Speak Frankly," *Army*, September 1977, 4.

Muhlenfeld, William F., Major, USA. "Our Embattled ROTC," *Army*, February 1969.

O'Sharron. "A Partial Solution to the Army's Honesty Problem," *Armed Forces Journal International*, January 1978, 25. (O'Sharron is the pen name of an Army officer.)

Patte, Chris, Colonel, USA. "Who Goes to Senior Service Schools?" *Army*, April 1975, 41–48.

Rostow, Walt W. "The Domestic Determinants of Foreign Policy or the Tocqueville Oscillation," *Naval War College Review*, September 1970, 4.

Rowe, James N., Major, USA. "How I Survived," *Army Digest*, May 1971.

Rusk, Dean. "Dean Rusk: On the Presidency," *New York Times*, 23 March 1971, 37C.

Smith, Robert H., Captain, USN. "A United States Navy for the Future," *US Naval Institute Proceedings*, March 1971, 18–25.

Sorley, Lewis, Lt. Colonel, USA (Ret.). "The Body Count Revisited," *Armed Forces Journal International*, November 1977, 25.

Sparrow, Herbert G., Major General, USA (Ret.). "Cheating at West Point—Who Are the Losers?" *Officer Review*, November 1965, 6–7.

_____. "Courage When Bricks Are Falling," Letters to the Editor Page, *Washington Star*, 2 January 1977.

_____. "The Promises Men Live By," *Armed Forces Journal International*, May 1975, 21–22.

Taylor, Maxwell D., "Military Advice—Its Use in Government," *Vital Speeches*, 18 March 1964, 336–339.

_____. "Holding Strategy," *Washington Post*, 4 February 1966, A8.

Timmes, Charles J., Major General, USA (Ret.). "The Naive Years," *Army*, May 1977, 35–40.

White, Thomas, General, USAF (Ret.). "The Impossible Role of the Joint Chiefs," *Newsweek*, 11 June 1962, 28.

Woodward, C. Vann. "The Age of Reinterpretation," *American Historical Review*, 66, October 1960, 1–19.

Government Documents

Collins, James Lawton, Jr., Brigadier General, USA. *Vietnam Studies: The Development and Training of the South Vietnam Army, 1950–1972.* Department of the Army, 1974.

Congressional Record, 124, 10 February 1978.

Department of the Army. DACS-MA. Memorandum for Lt. General Forsythe; Subject: Enhanced Professionalism: Corrective Actions Based on the AWC

Bibliography

Professionalism Study, Tab B, 6–7. Headquarters, Department of the Army, 6 October 1971.

Department of the Army. *The Modern Volunteer Army: A Program for Professionals*, 1971.

Department of the Army. "Guide to the Reserve Components," Pamphlet 135–3. Headquarters, Department of the Army, July 1977.

Heiser, Joseph M., Lt. General, USA. *Vietnam Studies: Logistic Support*. Department of the Army, 1974.

Johnson, Lyndon B. "Toward Peace with Honor." Press conference statement. The White House, 28 July 1965.

Johnson, Lyndon B., Robert S. McNamara and Dean Rusk. *Why Vietnam?* Department of State, 20 August 1965.

Kennedy, John F. *Public Papers of the Presidents: John F. Kennedy*. Government Printing Office, 1963.

Larsen, Stanley R., Lt. General, USA and James Lawton Collins, Jr., Brigadier General, USA. *Vietnam Studies: Allied Participation in Vietnam*. Department of the Army, 1975.

Larsen, Stanley R., Lt. General, USA (Ret.). US Army War College Senior Officer Debriefing Program, Transcript of 7 January 1977.

Marshall, S.L.A., Brigadier General, USAR (Ret.). *The Armed Forces Officer*. U.S. Department of Defense (DOD GEN-36), MS.

McNamara, Robert S. "The Tasks of Defense." Statement before Defense Subcommittee of the Senate Appropriations Committee. U.S. Department of Defense, 4 August 1965.

Modern Volunteer Army Staff Document. "An Army People Want," Lt. Colonel Peter M. Dawkins, The Pentagon, 1972.

Modern Volunteer Army Staff Paper. "Recommended Plan of Attack—AWC Study— Background Data," 2.

Modern Volunteer Army Staff Working Paper. "AWC Professionalism Study— Background Data and Need for Chief of Staff Attention," 1.

Nixon, Richard M. *US Foreign Policy for the 1970s*. United States Government Printing Office, 1970.

Rusk, Dean. *The Tasks of Diplomacy*. United States Department of State, 3 September 1965.

Sharp, U. S. Grant, Admiral, USN. *Report on the War in Vietnam: Section I, Report on Air and Naval Campaigns Against North Vietnam Command—Wide Support of the War, June 1964–July 1968*. United States Government Printing Office, 1969.

TFX Contract Investigation, Permanent Subcommittee on Investigations, Committee on Government Operations, United States Senate. Washington, D.C., 1963.

Tolson, John J., Lt. General, USA. *Vietnam Studies: Air Mobility*. United States Government Printing Office, 1973.

United States Air Force, *Southeast Asia Monograph Series*. Vols. I, II, and III. United States Government Printing Office.

United States Army War College. *Study on Military Professionalism*. USAWC, 1970.

United States Code. Title 10, Chapter 5.

United States Command Information Spotlight—Lt. Colonel Herbert—United States Army Command Information Unit. Washington, D.C., Vol. 21, 12 November 1971.

United States Department of Defense. *United States-Vietnam Relations 1945–1967*. United States Government Printing Office, 1971. Vols. 4, 5, 6.

Bibliography

United States Department of State. *Aggression from the North: The Record of North Vietnam's Campaign to Conquer South Vietnam*. Publication 7839. United States Government Printing Office, February 1965.

United States Joint Chiefs of Staff. *Publication Number Four*, July 1969.

United States Military Academy. *Register of Graduates*. R. R. Donnelley & Sons, Company, 1971.

Westmoreland, William C., General, USA. *Report on the War in Vietnam: Section II, Report on Operations in South Vietnam, January 1964–June 1968*. United States Government Printing Office, 1969.

Yarborough, William P., Lt. General, USA (Ret.). United States Army War College, Senior Officer Debriefing Program, Transcript of Tape Two, 18–19.

Published Studies

Braestrup, Peter. *Big Story*, two volumes. Westview Press, 1977.

Hamilton, William A., Ph.D. "Vietnam Reportage: Media Standards and Journalistic Accountability." *Tenth World Media Conference*, Washington, D.C., 22–25 March 1989.

The International Institute for Strategic Studies. *The Military Balance, 1975–1976*. IISS, 1975.

Johnson, Robert B. "Tactical Warfare and the Limited War Dilemma," *TEMPO Review Paper*, General Electric, 1961.

Lavalle, A. J. C., Major (ed.). *The Tale of Two Bridges and the Battle for the Skies Over North Vietnam*, Dept. of the Air Force, 1976.

Lefever, Ernest W. *TV and National Defense: An Analysis of CBS News, 1972–1973*. Institute for American Strategy, 1974.

Montague, Robert M., Jr. *Pacification: The Overall Strategy in South Vietnam*. United States Army War College, 1966.

Newhouse, John, et al. *US Troops in Europe*. The Brookings Institution, 1971.

Sparrow, Herbert G., Major General, USA. *Report of the Personnel Service Support Systems Group, PS3 Study*, Department of the Army, 1972.

Thompson, W. Scott, and Donaldson D. Frizzell. *The Lessons of Vietnam*, Crane, Russak & Co., 1977.

Unpublished Papers

Eccles, Henry E., Rear Admiral, USN (Ret.). "A Vietnam Commentary." United States Naval War College, 1964–1970.

_____. "The Vietnam Hurricane on the Pentagon in the Eye of the Storm." The George Washington University Logistics Research Project, June 1969.

Fulluo, C.M., Lt. Colonel, USA. "The Soldier Union Threat to the Army." 1 August 1975.

Keeley, John B. "The Military and Management—Professions in Conflict." 4 January 1978.

"U.S. Army Dental Corps in Vietnam." United States Army Health Systems Command.

Vann, John Paul. "Harnessing the Revolution in Vietnam." Circa 1964.

Speeches, Lectures, Radio and Television Broadcasts

Gorman, Paul F., Major General, USA. "Vietnam and After: The U.S. Army, 1976." A Lecture at the University of New Brunswick, Fredericton, Canada, 9 February 1977.

Bibliography

Maclear, Michael, "The Ten Thousand Day War, Vietnam, 1945–1975," a 13-part series broadcast on Canadian television in 1980.

Piao, Lin. "Long Live the Victory of the People's War." Foreign Broadcast Information Service Daily Report, No. 171 (45), 3 September 1965, 1–33.

"Reflections on a Revolution." *Bill Moyer's Journal*. WNET New York, 22 February 1976.

Roberts, Michael. "The Military Revolution 1560–1630." An Inaugural Lecture before the Queen's University of Belfast. Marjory Boyd, M.A., n.d.

Westmoreland, William C., General, USA (Ret.). "Vietnam in Perspective." Delivered to the Indianapolis Chapter of the Association of the United States, 20, 29 July 1977, 1–6.

Secondary Sources

Books and Dissertations

Abel, Elie. *The Missile Crisis.* New York: Bantam Books, 1968.

Adler, Selig. *The Isolationist Impulse.* London; New York: Abelard-Schuman, Ltd., 1957.

Allen, Frederick Lewis. *Only Yesterday.* New York: Harper & Row, 1931.

Alsop, Stewart. *The Center.* New York: Harper & Row, 1968.

Ambrose, Stephen E. *Upton and the Army.* Baton Rouge: Louisiana State University Press, 1964.

Ardrey, Robert. *The Territorial Imperative.* New York: Atheneum, 1966.

Arendt, Hannah. *Crises of the Republic.* New York: Harcourt Brace Jovanovich, 1972.

Armbruster, Frank, et al. *Can We Win in Vietnam?* Westport, CT: Praeger, 1968.

Aron, Raymond. *The Century of Total War.* Boston: Beacon Press, 1954.

_____. *The Imperial Republic.* Cambridge, MA: Winthrop Publishers, Inc., 1974.

Art, Robert J. *The TFX Decision.* New York: Little, Brown & Co., 1968.

Baldwin, Hanson W. *Strategy for Tomorrow.* New York: Harper & Row, 1970.

Barnet, Richard J. *Intervention and Revolution.* New York: Mentor Books, 1972.

Benet, Stephen Vincent. *John Brown's Body.* New York: Holt, Rinehart & Winston, 1968.

Berger, W. E. "The Role of the Armed Services in International Policy." Unpublished Doctoral dissertation, University of Nebraska–Lincoln, February 1956.

Birnbaum, Karl E. *Peace in Europe.* Oxford, UK: Oxford University Press, 1970.

Birnbaum, Karl E. in W. Stahl's (ed.) *The Politics of Postwar Germany*, Westport, CT: Praeger, 1961.

Blaik, Earl. *You Have to Pay the Price.* New York: Holt, Rinehart & Winston, 1960.

Blaufarb, Douglas S. *The Counter-Insurgency Era: US Doctrine and Performance 1950 to the Present.* New York: The Free Press, 1977.

Bloodworth, Dennis. *An Eye for the Dragon.* New York: Farrar, Straus & Giroux, 1970.

Borklund, Carl W. *Men of the Pentagon.* Westport, CT: Praeger, 1966.

Bracher, Karl Dietrich. *The German Dictatorship.* Westport, CT: Praeger, 1970.

Brandon, Henry. *Anatomy of Error.* London: Gambit, Inc., 1969.

Brodie, Bernard. *War and Politics.* New York: Macmillan, 1973.

Bullock, Allan. *Hitler: A Study in Tyranny.* New York: Bantam Books, 1961.

Burns, James MacGregor. *Roosevelt: The Lion and the Fox.* New York: Harcourt Brace and World, Inc., 1956.

Bibliography

Burruss, L. H. "Bucky," Lt. Colonel, USA (Ret.) *Heart of the Storm: A Novel of Men and Women in the Gulf War.* iUniverse, 2000.

Buttinger, Joseph. *Vietnam: A Political History.* Westport, CT: Praeger, 1968.

Calleo, David. *The Atlantic Fantasy.* Baltimore: The Johns Hopkins Press, 1970.

Caro, Robert A. *Lyndon Johnson: Means of Ascent.* New York: Vintage Books, 1991.

_____. *Master of the Senate.* New York: Vintage Books, 2009.

_____. *The Passage of Power.* New York: Vintage Books, 2013.

Childs, David. *Germany Since 1918.* New York: Harper & Row, 1970.

Coombs, Philip H. *The Fourth Dimension of Foreign Policy.* New York: Harper & Row, 1964.

Cooper, Chester L. *The Lost Crusade.* New York: Dodd, Mead & Co., 1970.

Croft-Cooke, Rupert. *Conduct Unbecoming.* Simon & Schuster, 1975.

de Gaulle, Charles, Captain, French Army. *Vers l'Armée de Métier.* Paris: Librairie Plon, 1971. (Originally published in 1934.)

Douhet, Giulio. *Makers of Modern Strategy.* (ed.) Edward Mead Earle. New York: Athenium, 1967.

Emerson, William R. "F.D.R." in Ernest R. May's, *The Ultimate Decision*, New York: George Braziller, 1960, 133–177.

Esposito, Vincent J., Colonel, USA. *The West Point Atlas of American Wars.* Westport, CT: Praeger, 1959.

Evans, Rowland, and Robert Novak. *Lyndon B. Johnson: The Exercise of Power.* New York: Signet Books, 1966.

Fall, Bernard. *Street without Joy.* Mechanicsburg, PA: Stackpole Books, 1963.

_____. *The Two Vietnams.* Westport, CT: Praeger, 1963.

Fishel, Wesley R. (ed.). *Vietnam: The Anatomy of a Conflict.* Itasca, IL: F.E. Peacock Publishing, Inc., 1968.

Fitzgerald, Francis. *Fire in the Lake.* New York: Little, Brown & Co., 1972.

Fliess, Peter J. *Thucydides and the Politics of Bipolarity.* Baton Rouge: Louisiana State University Press, 1966.

Furguson, Ernest B. *Westmoreland: The Inevitable General.* New York: Little, Brown & Co., 1968.

Galbraith, John Kenneth. *The Affluent Society.* New York: Houghton Mifflin, 1958.

_____. *The New Industrial State.* New York: Houghton Mifflin, 1969.

Galloway, K. Bruce, and R. B. Johnson, Jr. *West Point: America's Power Fraternity.* New York: Simon & Schuster, 1973.

Gardner, John W. *Excellence.* New York: Harper & Row, 1961.

Gavin, James M., Lt. General, USA (Ret.). *Crisis Now.* New York: Random House, 1968.

_____. *War and Peace in the Space Age.* New York: Harper & Brothers, 1958.

Goldstein, Joseph, Bruce Marshall, and Jack Schwartz. *The My Lai Massacre and Its Cover-Up: Beyond the Reach of Law.* New York: The Free Press, 1976.

Graebner, Norman A. (ed.). *Ideas and Diplomacy.* Baltmore: Beacon Press, 1964.

_____. *Manifest Destiny.* Indianapolis: Bobbs Merrill, 1968.

Graff, Henry F. *The Tuesday Cabinet.* Upper Saddle River, NJ: Prentice-Hall, 1970.

Halberstam, David. *The Best and the Brightest.* New York: Random House, 1972.

_____. *The Making of a Quagmire.* New Yorl: Random House, 1964.

Halperin, Morton H. *Defense Strategies for the Seventies.* New York: Little, Brown & Co., 1971.

Hamilton, William A., Ph.D. "The Decline and Fall of the Joint Chiefs of Staff." In *War, Strategy, and Maritime Power* by B. M. Simpson III, 295. New Brunswick, NJ: Rutgers University Press, 1977.

Bibliography

Hanson, Victor Davis. *The Second World Wars: How the First Global Conflict was Fought and Won.* New York: Basic Books, 2017.

Hartmann, Frederick H. *The Relations of Nations.* 3d ed. Macmillan, 1967.

Helmer, John. *Bringing the War Home.* New York: The Free Press, 1974.

Hoffman, Stanley. *Gulliver's Troubles.* New York: McGraw-Hill, 1968.

Homze, Edward L. *Arming the Luftwaffe.* Lincoln: University of Nebraska Press, 1976.

Hornbeck, Stanley K. *The United States and the Far East.* World Peace Foundation, 1942.

Huntington, Samuel P. *The Common Defense.* New York: Columbia University Press, 1961.

_____. *The Soldier and the State.* New York: Vintage Books, 1957.

Janowitz, Morris. *The Professional Soldier.* New York: The Free Press, 1960.

Janowitz, Morris (ed.). *The New Military.* New York: Russell Sage Foundation, 1964.

Just, Ward. *Military Men.* New York: Alfred A. Knopf, 1970.

Kalb, Marvin, and Elie Abel. *Roots of Involvement.* New York: W.W. Norton & Co., Inc. 1971.

Kaplan, Morton A. (ed.). *Great Issues of International Politics.* London: Aldine Publishing Company, 1970.

Kaufmann, William W. *The McNamara Strategy.* New York: Harper & Row, 1964.

Keegan, John. *The Face of Battle.* London: Cox & Wyman, Ltd., 1976.

Keeley, John B. (ed.). *The All Volunteer Force and American Society.* Charlottesville: University of Virginia Press, 1978.

Kissinger, Henry A. *The Necessity for Choice.* New York: Harper & Brothers, 1961.

_____. *The Troubled Partnership.* McGraw-Hill, 1965.

Korb, Lawrence J. *The Joint Chiefs of Staff: The First Twenty-five Years.* Bloomington: Indiana University Press, 1976.

Kovrig, Bennett. *The Myth of Liberation.* Baltimore: The Johns Hopkins University Press, 1973.

Kuniczak, W. S. *The Thousand Hour Day.* New York: The Dial Press, 1966.

Lafeber, Walter. *America, Russia and the Cold War, 1945–1966.* Hoboken, NJ: John Wiley & Sons, 1967.

_____. *The New Empire.* Ithaca, NY: Cornell University Press, 1963.

Lartéguy, Jean. *The Centurions.* London: Hutchinson, 1961.

_____. *The Praetorians.* London: Hutchinson, 1963.

Lazo, Mario. *Dagger in the Heart.* New York: Funk & Wagnalls, 1968.

Liddell Hart, B. H. *The Strategy of the Indirect Approach.* Westport, CT: Praeger, 1954.

Link, Arthur S. *Woodrow Wilson and the Progressive Era.* New York: Harper & Brothers, 1954.

Loory, Stuart H. *Defeated.* New York: Random House, 1973.

Mackinder, H. J. "The Geographical Pivot of History," in *Democratic Ideals and Reality.* National Defense University Press, 1966.

Mahan, A.T. *The Influence of Sea Power on History.* 1660–1805. Mineola, NY: Dover Publications, 1987.

May, Ernest R. (ed.). *The Ultimate Decision.* New York: George Braziller, 1960.

McMaster, H. R. *Dereliction of Duty: Johnson, McNamara, the Joint Chiefs of Staff, and the Lies That Led to Vietnam.* New York: Harper Perennial, 1998.

Merk, Frederick. *Manifest Destiny and Mission in American History.* New York: Knopf, 1963.

_____. *The Monroe Doctrine and American Expansion.* New York: Knopf, 1966.

Meyerhoff, Arthur E. *The Strategy of Persuasion.* New York: Coward-McCann, Inc., 1967.

Bibliography

Middleton, Drew. *Can America Win the Next War?* New York: Charles Scribner's Sons, 1975.

Miller, Perry. *Errand into the Wilderness.* New York: Harper & Brothers, 1956.

Millis, Walter. *Arms and Men.* New York: Mentor Books, 1956.

Mills, C. Wright. *The Power Elite.* Oxford, NY: Oxford University Press, 1959.

Mollenhoff, Clark R. *The Pentagon.* New York: G. P. Putnam's Sons, 1967.

Morgenthau, Hans J. *A New Foreign Policy for the United States.* Westport, CT: Praeger, 1969.

Morison, Elting E. *Men, Machines and Modern Times.* Cambridge, MA: M.I.T. Press, 1966.

Mylander, Maureen. *The Generals.* New York: The Dial Press, 1974.

Myrer, Anton. *Once an Eagle.* New York: Holt, Rinehart & Winston, 1968.

The Officer's Guide. The Military Service Publishing Co., 1930.

Paterson, Thomas G. *Soviet-American Confrontation.* Baltimore: The Johns Hopkins University Press, 1973.

Perkins, Dexter. *A History of the Monroe Doctrine.* New York: Little, Brown & Co., 1963.

Peter, Laurence J. *The Peter Prescription.* New York: William Morrow & Co., Inc., 1972.

Peter, Laurence J., and Raymond Hall. *The Peter Principle.* New York: William Morrow & Co., Inc., 1969.

Pike, Douglas C. *The Viet Cong.* Cambridge, MA: M.I.T. Press, 1966.

Polmar, Norman. *Strategic Weapons.* Crane, Russak & Co., Inc., 1975.

Pusey, Merlo J. *The Way We Go to War.* New York: Houghton Mifflin, 1969.

Raymond, Jack. *Power at the Pentagon.* New York: Harper & Row, 1964.

Reston, James. *The Artillery of the Press.* New York: Harper & Row, 1966.

Rivers, William L. *The Opinion Makers.* New York: Beacon Press, 1967.

Roberts, Andrew. *Churchill: Walking with Destiny.* New York: Viking Press, 2018.

Roherty, James M. *Decisions of Robert S. McNamara.* Coral Gables, FL: University of Miami Press, 1970.

Sapin, Burton. *The Making of US Foreign Policy.* Washington, D.C.: The Brookings Institution, 1966.

Schelling, Thomas C. *Arms and Influence.* New Haven, CT: Yale University Press, 1966.

_____. *The Strategy of Conflict.* Cambridge, MA: Harvard University Press, 1960.

Schlesinger, Arthur M., Jr. *The Crisis of the Old Order.* Cambridge, MA: The Riverside Press, 1957.

_____. *Vietnam: The Bitter Heritage.* New York: Houghton Mifflin, 1966.

Sheehan, Neil, Hedrick Smith, E. W. Kenworthy, and Fox Butterfield (eds.). *The Pentagon Papers.* New York: Bantam Books, Inc., 1971.

Sherrill, Robert. *The Accidental President.* New York: Grossman, 1967.

Shy, John. *A People Numerous and Armed.* London: Oxford University Press, 1976.

Sidey, Hugh. *A Very Personal Presidency.* New York: Atheneum, 1968.

Sorley, Lewis. *A Better War: The Unexamined Victories and the Final Tragedy of America's Last Years in Vietnam.* New York: Harvest, 1999.

_____. *Honorable Warrior: General Harold K. Johnson and the Ethics of Command.* Lawrence: The University of Kansas Press, 1998.

_____. *Thunderbolt: General Creighton Abrams and the Army of His Times.* Bloomington: University of Indiana Press, 2008.

Speer, Albert. *Inside the Third Reich.* New York: Macmillan, 1970.

Bibliography

Spinks, Charles N., John C. Durr, and Stephen Peters. *The North Vietnamese Regime Institutions and Problems*. Washington, D.C.: The American University, 1969.
Steel, Roland. *Pax Americana*. New York: The Viking Press, 1967.
Steinberg, Alfred. *Sam Johnson's Boy*. New York: Macmillan, 1968.
Steyn, Mark. *America Alone: The End of the World as We Know It*. Washington, D.C.: Regnery Publishing, 2006.
Talese, Gay. *The Kingdom and the Power*. New York: World Publishing Company, 1969.
Tierney, Brian, Donald Kagan, and L. Pearce Williams. *Feudalism—Cause or Cure of Anarchy?* New York: Random House, 1967.
Trewhitt, Henry L. *McNamara*. New York: Harper & Row, 1971.
Tuchman, Barbara W. *The Guns of August*. New York: Random House, 1962.
Tuchman, Barbara W. *The March of Folly: From Troy to Vietnam*. New York: Alfred A. Knopf, 1984.
_____. *Stilwell and the American Experience in China, 1911–1945*. New York: Macmillan, 1970.
Tucker, Robert W. *The Radical Left and American Foreign Policy*. Baltimore: The Johns Hopkins University Press, 1971.
Tuveson, Ernest Lee. *The Redeemer Nation*. The University of Chicago Press, 1974.
Ulam, Adam B. *The Rivals*. New York: Viking Press, 1971.
Van Alstyne, Richard W. *The Rising American Empire*. New York: Quadrangle Books, 1965.
Varg, Paul A. *Foreign Policies of the Founding Fathers*. New York: Penguin Books, 1970.
Vazsonyi, Balint. *America's 30 Years War: Who Is Winning?* Washington, D.C.: Regnery Publishing, 1998.
Ward, Geoffrey C., and Ken Burns. *The Vietnam War: An Intimate History*. New York: Knopf, 2017.
Watt, Richard M. *The Kings Depart: The Tragedy of Germany—Versailles and the German Revolution*. London: Weidenfeld & Nicolson, 1969
Weigley, Russell F. *The American Way of War*. New York: Macmillan, 1973.
_____. *History of the United States Army*. New York: Macmillan, 1967.
Weinberg, Albert Katz. *Manifest Destiny*. Baltimore: The Johns Hopkins Press, 1935.
Wheeler, Tom. *Mr. Lincoln's T-Mails: How Abraham Lincoln Used the Telegraph to Win the Civil War*. New York: HarperCollins, 2006.
White, Theodore H. *The Making of the President 1968*. New York: Atheneum, 1969.
_____. *The Making of the President 1972*. New York: Atheneum, 1973.
Williams, William A. *The Tragedy of American Diplomacy*. New York: Dell Publishing Company, 1962.
Williams, William A. (ed.). *From Colony to Empire*. Hoboken, NJ: John Wiley & Sons, Inc., 1972.
Wilson, Sloan. *The Man in the Gray Flannel Suit*. New York: Simon & Schuster, 1955.
Winks, Robin W. *The Historian as Detective*. New York: Harper Colophon Books, 1970.

Articles and Periodicals

Alsop, Stewart, "Worse Than My Lai." *Newsweek*, 24 May 1971.
"Army Orders Herbert Not to Speak to the Media." *San Francisco Chronicle*, 5 November 1971.

Bibliography

Baldwin, Hanson W. "Kennedy Shapes Pentagon Ties." *New York Times*, 2 July 1961, Section IV, 5:1.

_____. "The McNamara Monarchy." *Saturday Evening Post*, 9 March 1963.

_____. "Westy's Side: His Memoirs of a Bitter War." *Army*, January 1976, 56–58.

Berry, F. Clifton, Jr. "A General Tells Why the Army Is Its Own Worst Enemy." *Armed Forces Journal International*, July 1977, 22.

"Black Power in Viet Nam." *Time*, 19 September 1969.

"Brown Zeros in on Benefits Erosion." *Army Times*, 13 February 1978, 20.

Burciaga, John. "Confessions of a Vietnam General." *Atlanta Constitution*, 4, 27 March 1976, 1, 13–14,

Butterfield, Fox. "Hanoi General Surprised at Speed of Saigon's Collapse." *New York Times*, 26 April 1976, 1, 16.

Cimbala, Stephen J. "New Myths and Old Realities: Defense and Its Critics." *World Politics*, October 1971, 127–157.

Darnton, Byron. "Rep. Johnson Sees Airmen in Action." *New York Times*, 10 June 1942.

"A Day in a Dwindling War." *Newsweek*, 13 September 1971.

"District Duns Davison for $14,000 in Taxes." *Army Times*, 8 January 1975, 18. (Refers to Major General Frederick Davison, USA (Ret.) and not General Michael J. Davison, USA (Ret.).)

"Down with Up or Out." Editorial from the *Army Times*, 6 March 1978, 15.

Elliott, Ward. "Are We Trying to Stop the Machine by Getting Rid of the Brakes?" *Army*, February 1971.

"End of the Youth Culture." *US News and World Report*, 3 October 1977, 54–56.

Ewing, Lee. "Excerpts from Hanoi General's Account of Drive." *New York Times*, 26 April 1976, 16.

_____. "It Can Happen Here." *Army Times*, 18 August 1971.

Fleming, Thomas. "Letter to a Professional Soldier." *Army*, February 1971.

Gavin, James M., Lt. General, USA (Ret.). "A Communication on Vietnam." *Harper's*, February 1966, 16–21.

Geyer, Georgie Anne. "The Military and the Memory of Vietnam." *Virginian-Pilot*, 20 June 1977, 16.

"Gore Would Oust the Joint Chiefs." *New York Times*, 20 May 1961, 1:5.

Graebner, Norman A. "America in the World." *The National Observer*, 27 March 1976, B5.

Hannah, Norman. "Vietnam: Now We Know." *National Review*, June 1976, 612–616.

"In the Courts: The Government vs. the Press." *Newsweek*, 28 June 1971.

Janis, Irving L. "Groupthink." *Psychology Today*, November 1971, 43–44, 46, 74–76.

Just, Ward S. "Soldiers." *Atlantic*, Part I, October 1970, 59–98, Part II, November 1970, 59–90.

Lazo, Mario, Sr. "Decision for Disaster." *Reader's Digest*, September 1974, 241–244.

"Lifetime Star Tenure May Halt 'Muzzling.'" *Army Times*, 6 March 1978, 10.

Lind, William S. "Should We Shoot an Admiral?" *Washington Star*, 25 July 1977, A-13.

Livingston, Gordon. "Letter from a Vietnam Veteran." *Saturday Review*, 20 September 1969.

Long, William F., Jr. "Counterinsurgency Revisited." *Naval War College Review*, November 1968, 4–10.

Marshall, S.L.A. "Motivation in Combat." *Infantry*, September-October 1970.

"Morale So Bad GI's Don't Care What Happens." *San Antonio Express*, 13 January 1971.

Mulligan, Hugh A. "Men at Arms: Time of Change." *San Antonio Express*, 23 May 1971.

159

Bibliography

Murphy, Charles J. V. "Cuba: The Record Set Straight." *Fortune*, September 1961, 92.

Namier, Sir Lewis B. "Symmetry and Repetition" in *Conflicts: Studies in Contemporary History*, Macmillan & Co., Ltd., 1942, 69–70.

Norford, Richard F. "Systems Analysis: A Missing Element in Foreign Policy Planning." *Naval War College Review*, January 1971, 80–100.

"President Poses with Joint Chiefs." *New York Times*, 28 May 1961, 39:5.

Reeves, Richard. "Media: Fallibility and the Fourth Estate." *Esquire*, February 1978, 8, 12.

Robinson, William H., Jr. "An Element of International Affairs—The Military Mind." *Naval War College Review*, November 1970, 4–15.

Saar, John. "You Can't Just Hand Out Orders." *Life*, 23 October 1970.

Schemmer, Benjamin. "How Much Is Enough? Tells a Lot ... But Not Enough," *Armed Forces Journal*, 1 February 1971, 36.

"Service to the Nation." *The National Guardsman*, April 1970, 22–29.

"71 Point Graduates Avoid Big 4 Arms." *Army Times*, 14 April 1977.

Shy, John. "The American Military Experience: History and Learning." *The Journal of Inter-Disciplinary History*, Winter 1971, 205–228

Silverman, Jerry M., and Peter M. Jackson. "Terror in Insurgency Warfare." *Military Review*, October 1970, 61–67.

Simmons, Ted. "Vietnam Army Officer Plans to Charge Two Superiors with Dereliction of Duty." *Salt Lake Tribune*, 13 March 1971.

Smith, Paul. "Airlift Hearing Sparks Debate on 'Muzzling.'" *Army Times*, 17 October 1977, 15.

"The Troubled US Army in Vietnam." *Newsweek*, 11 January 1971.

"TV Tells World War II as It Was." *Deseret News*, 7 April 1971.

von Hoffman, Nicholas. "Some Observations in Our Military's Remarkable Obedience to Civilian Masters." *Washington Post*, 30 March 1977.

Whiting, Allen S. "The Scholar and the Policy-Maker." *World Politics*, Spring 1972, 229–247.

"Would Oust Lemnitzer." *New York Times*, 5 June 1961, 3–4.

Index